Dominican Republic

Frontispiece: **Artwork**

Consultant: Edward Paulino, Department of Global History, CUNY/John Jay College, New York, NY

Please note: All statistics are as up-to-date as possible at the time of publication.

Book production by The Design Lab

Library of Congress Cataloging-in-Publication Data
Names: Rogers, Barbara Radcliffe, author. | Rogers Seavey, Lura, author.
Title: Dominican Republic : enchantment of the world / by Barbara Radcliffe
    Rogers and Lura Rogers Seavey.
Description: New York, NY : Children's Press, an imprint of Scholastic Inc.,
    2019. | Includes bibliographical references and index.
Identifiers: LCCN 2018019486 | ISBN 9780531126967 (library binding ; alk. paper)
Subjects: LCSH: Dominican Republic—Juvenile literature. | Dominican Republic.
Classification: LCC F1934.2 .R63 2019 | DDC 972.93—dc23
LC record available at https://lccn.loc.gov/2018019486

Scholastic Inc., 557 Broadway, New York, NY 10012

1 2 3 4 5 6 7 8 9 10 R 28 27 26 25 24 23 22 21 20 19

Dominican Republic

BY BARBARA RADCLIFFE ROGERS
AND LURA ROGERS SEAVEY

Enchantment of the World™
Second Series

CHILDREN'S PRESS®

An Imprint of Scholastic Inc.

Contents

Left to right: **Family,
dancers, beach,
parade, coral reef**

CHAPTER I

Welcome to Quisqueya

FIVE HUNDRED YEARS AGO, THE STEADY TRADE WINDS blew three tiny ships from Spain across the Atlantic Ocean. After briefly making landfall in the Bahamas, the ships landed on an island that the local people called Quisqueya but the Spanish would name Hispaniola. It was on this island that the Spanish would establish the first permanent European colony in the Americas. The modern nation of the Dominican Republic was part of this colony.

Hispaniola is located in an island chain called the West Indies, about 800 miles (1,300 kilometers) southeast of the U.S. state of Florida. The prevailing trade winds carried many other ships to Hispaniola, making it the gateway to the Caribbean and other parts of the Americas. The trade winds proved to be the winds of change, for the ships that rode the winds straight toward Hispaniola carried people, plants,

Opposite: **Traditional musicians perform for students in an old part of Santo Domingo, the capital of the Dominican Republic.**

A Dominican man rides his horse down the Yaque del Norte.

Old Island, New Names

The indigenous, or native, Taíno people who lived on Hispaniola when the Spanish arrived there called the island Quisqueya, meaning "mother of all lands." The Spanish conquerors claimed the island as their own, naming it La Isla Española, which means "the Spanish island." Over time, this was shortened to today's name, Hispaniola. Today, many people in the Dominican Republic continue to call the island Quisqueya. They consider the name imposed on them by conquerors to be offensive.

The Spanish did not rename all geographic features on the island. *Yaque*, the Taíno word for "river," was adopted by the Spanish to name the Yaque del Norte (North River) and Yaque del Sur (South River).

animals, and ideas that would change life there forever.

French ships came looking for a foothold in the Caribbean, and Europeans brought enslaved Africans to work on the plantations. The French and the Spanish fought over Hispaniola, and it took more than three hundred years for the Dominican people to break free of European control.

Over the years, the people of the Dominican Republic have struggled to overcome economic and political obstacles as they work toward making their country the best it can be. Some changes have come slowly, gradually altering the people and the nation, and sometimes changes have arrived as violently as the hurricanes that also seem to aim directly at the Dominican Republic's shore.

As you read about the Dominican Republic and its turbulent history, you will meet patriots, tyrants, baseball stars,

Bridges connect small islands off the Samaná Peninsula in the country's northeast. Known as the Bridges to Nowhere, they were constructed to bring visitors to a tourist site that was never built.

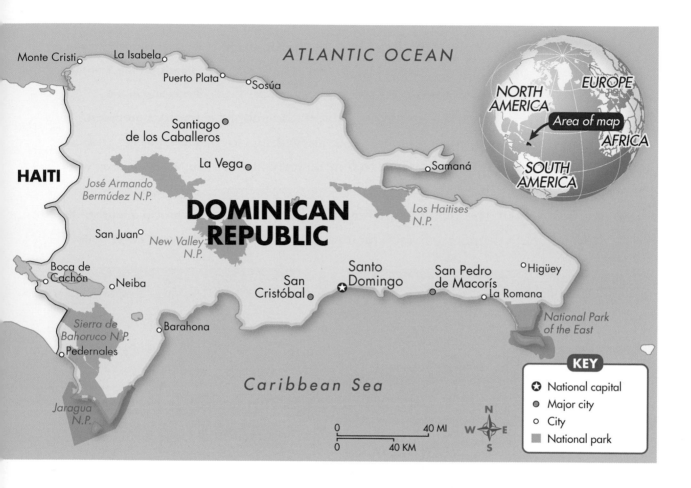

heroes, dictators, poets, pirates, and presidents. And you will meet a people who are deeply rooted in their families, their faith, and their little island country.

Many Americans know the Dominican Republic best for the long, white sand beaches that line the island's shores. These beaches draw millions of tourists each year who enjoy the tropical sun and refreshing breezes. Visitors also enjoy the vibrant culture and its joyous festivals like Carnival, a celebration held every winter.

But the Dominican Republic is much more than beaches and tourist complexes. Its landscapes include tall mountains, farmlands, mangrove swamps, and lakes. And its people are just as varied, a population with origins in Europe, Africa, the Caribbean, Asia, and elsewhere. People from these far-flung places have brought their culture, language, customs, music, and more, forming the rich mix that is the Dominican Republic today.

Children play on the beach in the southern Dominican Republic.

CHAPTER 2

Mountains in the Sea

THE DOMINICAN REPUBLIC OCCUPIES TWO-THIRDS of Hispaniola, the second-largest island in the West Indies. The rest of the island is the nation of Haiti. The Dominican Republic covers an area of 18,816 square miles (48,734 square kilometers), making it a little smaller than the U.S. states of Vermont and New Hampshire combined.

Hispaniola sits south of Florida, with the island of Cuba to the west and Puerto Rico to the east. All of these islands are the tops of a mountain chain called the Greater Antilles. The mountains rise from the ocean floor and separate the Atlantic Ocean to the north from the Caribbean Sea to the south.

The Lay of the Land

Hispaniola has a varied landscape that includes mountains, valleys, and sandy beaches. The central and western parts of

Opposite: **In some parts of the Dominican Republic, the mountains descend directly to the sea.**

The Father of Dominican Independence

Duarte Peak was named for Juan Pablo Duarte, the leader of the movement that freed Dominicans from Haitian rule. Duarte was raised by wealthy parents, and after spending many years studying in Europe, he returned to his home country determined to free his people from Haitian rule. After years of planning, Duarte's supporters were able to capture the city of Santo Domingo in 1844 and declare the Dominican Republic independent.

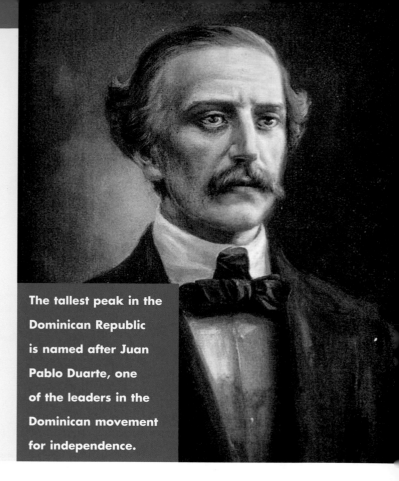

The tallest peak in the Dominican Republic is named after Juan Pablo Duarte, one of the leaders in the Dominican movement for independence.

the country are the most mountainous, while the eastern section of the island sits at a much lower elevation.

The largest and tallest mountain chain is the Cordillera Central, which stretches southeast across the center of the island to the Caribbean Sea. It is home to Duarte Peak, which at 10,417 feet (3,175 meters) above sea level is the country's tallest point and the highest in the Caribbean. In the north, the Cordillera Septentrional runs along the Atlantic coast from the Haitian border to the base of the Samaná Peninsula in the east. The peaks of this range are lower, reaching only about 3,300 feet (1,000 m).

A smaller range called Sierra de Neiba sits to the south of

Cordillera Central, and beyond that the Sierra de Bahoruco borders the Caribbean Sea. The eastern part of the island is home to the Cordillera Oriental, a chain of much smaller mountains that overlook rolling hills to the south. The terrain becomes gradually flatter and lower as it approaches the Caribbean coast.

Rivers, Valleys, and Lowlands

Most of the island's major waterways begin in the Cordillera Central. The country's longest river is the Yaque del Norte,

Many people trek to the spectacular El Limón Waterfall on the Samaná Peninsula and swim in the pool at its base.

This mosquito was trapped in pine resin about twenty-five million years ago. The resin eventually became amber.

The Amber Coast

The northern coast of the Dominican Republic is often called the Amber Coast because of the rich supply of amber that is found in the area. Amber is actually the fossil of ancient tree resin, the same type of sticky substance you see coming out of a pine tree. Millions of years ago, resin pooled and became buried in the ground or underwater, and over time the pressure changed it into a hard, yellow-orange nugget. Among the most interesting pieces of amber are those with insects suspended inside. The insects were trapped by the sticky resin and are perfectly preserved. The amber is mined from the coastal hills, polished and cleaned, and then sold to craftspeople who turn it into jewelry.

which begins near Duarte Peak and flows for 184 miles (296 km) until it reaches the Atlantic Ocean at the town of Monte Cristi. Along the way, this river supplies the water for the city of Santiago de los Caballeros and provides much-needed nutrients and irrigation for the farms of the Cibao Valley.

The Yaque del Sur flows south from the slopes of Duarte, starting at an elevation of 8,500 feet (2,600 m). It flows from the mountains and then through the San Juan Valley and Neiba Valley, finally emptying into the Caribbean Sea at the end of its 80-mile (130 km) journey.

The fertile Cibao Valley rests between the Cordillera Central and Cordillera Septentrional mountain ranges. The Yaque del Norte river provides water and nutrients to the valley's farmlands. This constant supply of water and rich sediment makes the Cibao Valley some of the country's most productive farmland. It is a major center for crops like grains and tobacco. The city of Santiago de los Caballeros sits in the middle of the Cibao Valley.

White-water rafting is popular on the Yaque del Norte River.

As Lake Enriquillo expands, trees are submerged and eventually die.

The Largest Lake, and Growing

Lake Enriquillo is the largest lake in the Caribbean, and it is getting bigger. In recent years, its surface area has been growing steadily. The lake doubled in size between 2003 and 2013.

The expansion of the lake has many scientists puzzled. Global climate change may be playing a role. As the climate warms, the ocean waters around the Dominican Republic also warm, which produces greater rainfall. The lake has no outlet, so most of the water that falls into the lake stays. Whether this accounts for all the lake's growth, however, remains uncertain.

As the lake grows, it is swallowing the farming town of Boca de Cachón, destroying homes and fields where crops like cassava root and banana are planted, as well as pastureland for cattle. It has also flooded several roads, including a main highway into Haiti. The flooding is also damaging to animal habitats, killing the trees where palm crows nest.

The Neiba Valley sits between the Sierra de Neiba and Sierra de Bahoruco ranges. Long ago these mountain ranges were separated by a stretch of sea. As the land changed over time, the salt water was trapped, resulting in the saline Lake Enriquillo and nearby Lake Saumâtre in Haiti. Water flowing from the Neiba Mountains feeds Enriquillo, the country's largest lake. The surface of Lake Enriquillo is the lowest point on the island of Hispaniola at 112 feet (34 m) below sea level during the drier months of the year.

Along the southern coast of the island, the land lies flat and low. Along this coastal plain are most of the nation's

Cactus grows in the dry lands along the southwestern coast.

Geographic Features of the Dominican Republic

Total Area: 18,816 square miles (48,734 sq km)

Length of Coastline: About 800 miles (1,300 km)

Highest Elevation: Duarte Peak, 10,417 feet (3,175 m) above sea level

Lowest Elevation: Lake Enriquillo, 112 feet (34 m) below sea level

Longest River: Yaque del Norte, 184 miles (296 km) long

Largest Lake: Enriquillo, 135 square miles (350 sq km)

Average High Temperature: 87°F (31°C) in July

Average Low Temperature: 67°F (19°C) in January

sugarcane fields. Cities such as Barahona in the southwest and San Pedro de Macorís in the southeast are important in the sugar industry. La Romana, also in the southeast, is lined with beautiful beaches and has a thriving tourist trade.

Also part of the Dominican Republic are several low-lying islands off the southern part of Hispaniola. Saona, off the southeastern tip, attracts many tourists with its beautiful beaches. Beata and Catalina are visited less.

Fishers leave their boats along the white sand shores of Saona Island.

Urban Landscapes

The largest city in the Dominican Republic is its capital, Santo Domingo, which has a population of about 2.9 million people. Santiago de los Caballeros, more commonly called Santiago, is the nation's second-largest city, with a population of approximately 550,000 people. The city was founded in 1494 by the Europeans and rebuilt closer to the Yaque del Norte after an earthquake in 1564. Sitting in the center of the Cibao Valley, Santiago is an important center for food processing. Important sites in the city include the Cathedral of Santiago el Mayor and the Monument to the Heroes of the Restoration.

The Dominican Republic's third- and fourth-largest cities, La Vega and San Cristóbal, respectively, each have about 210,000 residents.

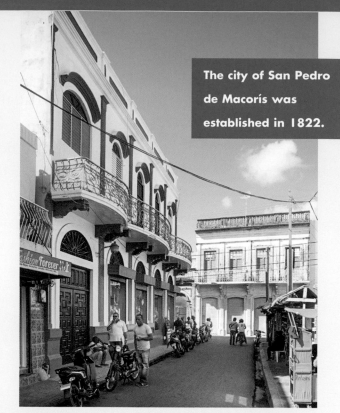

The city of San Pedro de Macorís was established in 1822.

La Vega was founded in 1495 by Bartholomew Columbus near the site of a fortress that had been built the previous year. San Cristóbal was founded in 1575 after gold was discovered nearby. Both are now important business centers in rich agricultural regions.

Home to about 206,000 people, San Pedro de Macorís is the nation's fifth-largest city. It sits on the southern shore of the eastern part of the country between the capital city of Santo Domingo and the city of La Romana. Convenient to the region's sugarcane fields, it is a center for sugar processing. It has also become a hub of baseball in the Dominican Republic and produces more professional players than any other city in the world.

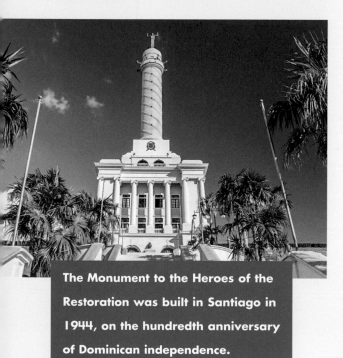

The Monument to the Heroes of the Restoration was built in Santiago in 1944, on the hundredth anniversary of Dominican independence.

Rainy and Warm

The climate of the Dominican Republic is tropical, with hot summers and warm winters. Higher elevations tend to have cooler weather, sometimes reaching down to freezing in winter, while the lowlands of the valleys and coast can reach over 100°F (38°C) in the summer months.

The amount of rain that falls varies depending on the time of year and the elevation. The rainy season runs from May through November. During this time, the mountains get far more rain than the lowlands. While the Cordillera Central may get over 100 inches (250 centimeters) per year, the city

Dominicans make their way through the hard rain of a summer storm.

A Dominican girl plays in the sea. Although a dip in the ocean can be refreshing, the water temperature is often nearly as warm as the air temperature.

of Santiago in the valley below gets less than 40 inches (100 cm) per year. The coastal plains receive between 40 and 60 inches (100 and 150 cm) annually, depending on elevation.

Heavy rainfall can overload rivers and streams. The rushing water causes soil erosion and carries the dirt downstream. This can cause dangerous mudslides. It also damages fragile coral reefs as the sediment is dumped into the sea. Heavy rain is also a major problem for farmers, as hillside plantations can be washed away and low-lying fields can flood.

In 1930, Hurricane San Zenón destroyed about half the buildings in Santo Domingo.

In the Path of Hurricanes

Each year during the summer and fall, huge swirling storms form in the Atlantic Ocean. If the sustained winds reach 74 miles (119 km) per hour, the storm is called a hurricane. The storms travel over the ocean in a southwesterly arc. The island of Hispaniola sits in the middle of this arc, making hurricanes a frequent threat. Their howling winds and pounding rain wreak havoc when they make landfall.

Although serious hurricanes hit Hispaniola an average of every two years, some have stood out in their destructiveness. In 1930, Hurricane San Zenón, one of the most destructive hurricanes in history, hit Santo

Domingo and killed as many as eight thousand people, injuring another fifteen thousand. In 1979, Hurricane David killed more than two thousand people and caused major flooding, destroying crops and homes.

Today, advance warning systems and public shelters help save many lives, but people are still at risk. The poorest citizens are the most affected because many live in structures that cannot withstand the wind. Those who live on hillsides are threatened by mudslides caused by the rainfall, and coastal communities are battered by high waves and tides.

CHAPTER 3

Natural Neighbors

THE DOMINICAN REPUBLIC IS A SMALL NATION, BUT it is home to a wide array of plants and animals. It has many different types of terrain, from towering mountains to broad beaches, allowing many different species to grow and thrive. It also has several ecosystems, including rain forests, deserts, and the delicate coastal waters. Many of the Dominican Republic's plants and animals are native to the region, while others were imported by Europeans.

Opposite: **The rhinoceros iguana is native to Hispaniola and nearby islands. The lizard, which grows up to 4.5 feet (1.4 m) long, earned its name from the bony growth on its snout.**

In the Mountains

About 5,600 species of plants can be found in the Dominican Republic. The highest elevations, which are the coolest places, have coniferous (cone-bearing) trees such as Hispaniolan pine. Forests once covered 70 percent of the island, but have been shrinking because of illegal logging. The New Valley

National Park lies high in the mountains in the center of the nation. It protects a large area of these trees from being cut down, preserving species and preventing deforestation.

Rain forests are found in the warmer, lower elevations of the mountainous areas. The rain forest is also in danger from logging because many of the trees that grow there are valuable hardwoods that can be sold at high prices. Ebony, mahogany, and satinwood trees have been almost completely removed from many sections of the rain forest.

Cedar and juniper also grow in the rain forest, as do food-bearing plants like guava, star apple, pepper, calabash, and

cashew. The more moderate regions are also home to trees such as Dominican magnolia and ceiba. Also known as silk-cotton trees, ceibas can live to be three hundred years old.

In the Desert

The hottest, driest areas are in the western part of the country near the border with Haiti. This is a semi-desert ecosystem where the plant life is limited to things like agave and cactus, which don't need a lot of water. The national flower is a cactus flower called the Bayahibe rose. These beautiful pink blooms are native only to the Dominican Republic.

Lake Enriquillo sits in a dry region at the edge of the southern border. It has an unusual ecosystem thanks to its salty water. The lake is home to species of saltwater fish that are unique to Hispaniola, including the Hispaniola pupfish. Living on the lake's island, Isla Cabritos, are the endangered Ricord's iguana and the threatened rhinoceros iguana.

A long root helps keep a yellow mombin tree erect in the Dominican forest. These trees produce an acidic, plumlike fruit.

Along the Coast

Tall native royal palms line many of the white sand beaches in the Dominican Republic's coastal regions. The coconut palm also grows along the water's edge, although it is not native to the region. Instead, it was imported from Africa. The liquid from inside the coconut is a popular Dominican drink.

Swampy coastal areas are where mangrove trees grow. These trees are important to the coastal ecosystem because their tangled roots hold soil in place that would otherwise be washed away by waves and tides. The protection the mangroves provide is especially important during strong storms when the shore is most at risk. The network of mangrove roots also makes a safe place for wildlife such as fish, sponges, and shrimp.

The fingerlike roots of the mangrove rise in a tangle above the water in Los Haitises National Park.

Preserving Nature

To help protect its remarkable natural diversity, the Dominican Republic has established many national parks. Jaragua National Park, in the southwest, is the largest protected area in all the Caribbean. It preserves dry forests, beaches, lagoons, and Beata Island. Manatees and dolphins swim in its protected waters.

In the interior, Sierra de Bahoruco National Park protects a wide variety of forests including cloud forest, a damp region perpetually covered in clouds. Many plants thrive in this park, including 180 different species of delicate

The broad-billed tody lives only in lowland regions on the island of Hispaniola, including in Sierra de Bahoruco National Park.

Los Haitises National Park protects many small limestone islands off the coast.

orchids. Another mountain park, José Armando Bermúdez National Park, protects the forests on the slopes of Duarte Peak.

Los Haitises National Park is located on the northeastern coast. It is famed for its dramatic limestone hills and caverns. Located in the southeast of the country is the National Park of the East. The park features incredible diversity. There are rain forests and waterfalls, beautiful beaches and tangled mangrove forests. It is the most visited national park in the Dominican Republic.

The water along the coast is also home to tiny animals called anthozoans. They produce calcium carbonate, which builds up to form the delicate coral reefs that support many different species of fish and sea creatures. The reefs serve as a protective barrier that keeps these smaller creatures from being attacked by the bigger deep-sea wildlife. Deforestation and increased rain are threatening the coral because the soil runoff damages the fragile structures.

Wildlife

Rodents such as the insect-eating solenodon and its relative the hutia are among the largest land mammals in the Dominican Republic, but they are close to extinction. More common is the agouti. These creatures, about the size of a small dog, are related to guinea pigs. They live in the woods and fields, gathering in large groups to eat fruit and leaves.

Colorful fish swim among the coral off the coast of the Dominican Republic.

The National Bird

The palmchat, the national bird of the Dominican Republic, is found only on the island of Hispaniola. The small birds naturally live in areas with scattered trees, but they have adapted well to living in cities. They often nest in palm trees or on telephone poles. Palmchats are very social birds. They often gather in large groups and chirp loudly.

Palmchats build a single large nest that is used by ten to thirty pairs of birds. The nest has a private chamber for each pair.

Many more birds than mammals live in the Dominican Republic. Ducks, herons, and egrets linger near the water. Ospreys and kestrels perch high in the trees as they wait to hunt. Among the trees are colorful birds such as the broad-billed tody, the Hispaniolan woodpecker, and the bay-breasted cuckoo. The vervain hummingbird lives in the damp forests. Only 2.5 inches (6 cm) long, it is one of the world's smallest birds.

Many reptiles also inhabit the country. Sea turtles such as leatherbacks and hawksbills nest along the beaches in the southwest. Geckos, anoles, iguanas, and other lizards rest in the sun. The largest snake found in the country is the Hispaniolan boa, which can grow up to 13 feet (4 m) long. The boa hunts by grabbing its prey with its teeth and then squeezing it to death.

Plants and Animals from Far Away

The Spanish introduced many crops to Hispaniola. This includes the country's biggest cash crop, sugarcane, along with bananas, mangoes, and coffee. Because the Spanish had explored all over the globe, the plants they brought to Hispaniola came from many different regions. Almonds were brought from India, breadfruit came from the islands of the South Pacific, and eucalyptus came from Australia. Citrus fruit and cocoa were imported from neighboring Central and South America, which the Spanish also conquered. Today, only around 35 percent of the island's plant species were there before the Europeans first landed.

Mangoes are native to Asia. They did not arrive in the Western Hemisphere until the 1700s.

The mongoose was introduced into Hispaniola in 1870 and quickly became a threat to native species.

Mongoose: Friend or Foe?

The mongoose is a small mammal known for being fearless, agile, and quick, all of which make it an expert hunter. After the Spanish introduced the mongoose to rid Hispaniola of its rat infestation, the aggressive creatures hunted native rodents and other small animals. They nearly drove the solenodon to extinction, and they diminished the populations of birds and iguanas. Mongooses, imported to get rid of pests, had become pests themselves.

The Spanish also introduced animals to Hispaniola, which disrupted the ecological balance of the island. Cows and pigs were imported as livestock, and horses and donkeys were brought over as work animals. Rats and mice soon adapted to the Caribbean habitat too, brought unintentionally on cargo ships. The rodent population grew quickly and became such a problem that the Spanish brought cats and mongooses to get rid of them, but these imports became a problem for native species because they had no natural predators on the island.

CHAPTER 4

A Journey Through Time

T HE FIRST HUMANS TO ARRIVE ON THE CARIBBEAN island of Hispaniola came from South America. They arrived between 4000 and 3000 BCE. It would be another three thousand years before another group, the Arawak, arrived from what is now Venezuela and established a colony on the island's easternmost tip. They named their settlement Quisqueya. Over time, more Arawak arrived, and some mixed with the original settlers who were farmers. This group began to call itself the Taíno, which means "good" or "noble," to distinguish themselves from the more aggressive Arawak. The more aggressive group eventually became known as the Caribs.

Taíno Culture

The Taíno occupied several Caribbean islands. They had developed a successful agricultural society. They grew corn,

Opposite: **Fort San Felipe was built in the mid-1500s to help protect Hispaniola's northern coast from pirates.**

cassavas, sweet potatoes, squash, and beans for food. They also cultivated tobacco, cotton for clothing, and the calabash gourd that was used to make containers to hold food and water. The Taíno also took advantage of the native plants that grew in their land. From the ceiba tree they made long canoes that could seat up to 150 people. They also constructed small houses from wood, which had thatched roofs made of straw.

Taíno society was organized into villages of one thousand to two thousand people. The village leader was a chief called a cacique, who could be either male or female. Individual villages were grouped into regional chiefdoms that also had leaders, much like modern government has leadership at both

Taíno leaders sat on a ceremonial seat called a *duho* during rituals in which they were said to communicate with spirits.

Taíno people painted these images of plants in a cave in eastern Hispaniola.

Pictures of the Past

The Taíno people did not have a written language. But they did make carvings and drawings, some of which have survived through the centuries. Softer surfaces like coral and limestone were used most often for carvings, and the light-colored walls of limestone caves still show images drawn more than two thousand years ago. Unfortunately, many of these caves were destroyed by mining operations before the government and private organizations stepped in to protect the ancient drawings.

a city and state level. Society was well organized, and the Taíno population on Hispaniola grew to at least half a million.

Another indigenous group was also vying for power in the Caribbean. The Carib people had originally come from what is now Venezuela, in northern South America. They were expert at making canoes, and they sailed to islands in the southern Caribbean, where they displaced the Taíno. By the

A Dominican man peels a papaya. The large fruit grows in clusters on a tree that looks like a palm.

Taíno Farming

Before the Europeans arrived, the Taíno people cultivated the calabash tree for its hard-shelled fruit. After eating the inside of the calabash, Taíno people dried the outer shell and used it to make containers, masks, tools, and utensils. The Taíno also farmed cassava, papaya, pepper, and tobacco, all of which are still grown by farmers in the Dominican Republic today.

late 1400s, the Caribs were sometimes attacking the Taíno on Hispaniola. But a more deadly enemy would soon arrive.

Invaders from the East

In 1492, three ships headed out from Spain under the leadership of explorer Christopher Columbus. The ships sailed across the Atlantic, reaching the island of Hispaniola in December. They established a settlement in what is now Haiti, called La Navidad. When Columbus returned the following year, he found the settlement destroyed. He founded a town he called

La Isabela farther east on the northern shore, in what is now the Dominican Republic. La Isabela became the Spanish base of operations in the Caribbean until Christopher's brother Bartholomew declared the town of Santo Domingo, on the southern shore, the new capital in 1496. The Spaniards had decided to focus their efforts to the south because they had heard there was more gold there. Santo Domingo would grow into a large city that became the political center of the Spanish empire as it expanded throughout the Americas.

The Spanish liked the island, which they named Hispaniola, for many reasons. It was centrally located in the Caribbean and was rich with valuable resources like gold. The Spanish also saw the Taíno people as a resource. The Spanish forced many Taínos to become laborers. The native people had to build, mine, and serve the Spanish. Soon, the Spanish monarchy imposed a system called *encomienda*, which granted the Spanish settlers rights to parcels of land and direct control over the Taíno people, making them a nation of slaves.

As more Spanish arrived, they began to fight among themselves. Just a few short years after it was first conquered, Hispaniola was in a civil war. When Spanish military leader Francisco de Bobadilla arrived in Santo Domingo in August

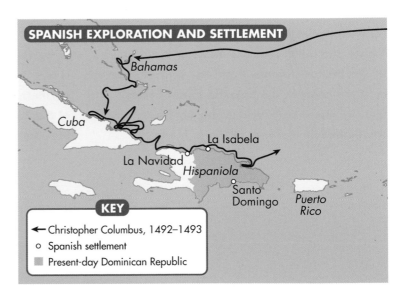

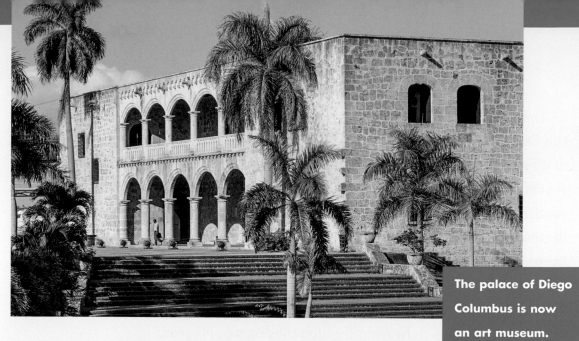

Historic Santo Domingo

Santo Domingo is the oldest permanent European settlement in the Americas. Ciudad Colonial (Spanish for "Colonial City"), the oldest neighborhood of Santo Domingo, has buildings dating from the early 1500s. One of these is often known as the Colonial Zone. It was the palace of the Columbus family, built by Christopher Columbus's son Diego in 1510. Today, the building looks much as it did when it was built. Columbus Park, the central square, is at the heart of the Colonial Zone. Beside it is the oldest cathedral in the Americas, the Cathedral of Santa María la Menor.

Construction began on the church in 1512, and it was completed in 1541.

The narrow cobblestone Calle Las Damas (Street of the Ladies) is the oldest paved street in the Americas, dating from 1502. Many of the city's historic landmarks are on this street, including the Ozama Fortress, which was built in 1502. Also on Calle Las Damas is the House of Bastidas, a sixteenth-century mansion, which is now home to a children's museum. At the northern end of the Colonial Zone are the ruins of the San Nicolás de Bari Hospital, the first hospital in the Western Hemisphere.

1500, he arrested Christopher and Bartholomew Columbus for failing as leaders and sent them back to Spain. Bobadilla took over and focused his attention on mining gold. Using indigenous laborers, he collected about 600 pounds (270 kg) of gold.

In 1502, he set sail with it to present it to the queen, but both he and the gold were lost at sea.

Hispaniola's next leader was Nicolás de Ovando, and he proved to be even more brutal and ruthless than the last. Under his rule, many Taínos died from abuse, and others committed suicide to escape the terrible conditions. His treatment of the local people was so harsh that many died

In 1500, Christopher Columbus was accused of tyranny, arrested, and sent back to Spain. The king of Spain soon ordered him released, however.

Francis Drake led English troops in battle against the Spanish for control of Santo Domingo in 1586.

and he soon began to import enslaved people from Africa to replace them.

One of the worst killers among the indigenous people was illness. They had never before been exposed to the diseases the Spanish carried, so their immune systems could not combat them. Within thirty years of Columbus's first landing, nearly all the Taíno people on the island had died.

After the end of Ovando's tyranny, Spain sent Christopher Columbus's son Diego to rule the colony at Hispaniola. To keep him from abusing his power, the Spanish Crown established a council called the *audiencia*, which reviewed his decisions and could challenge his policies. During his rule, Diego Columbus ordered the construction of the first European fortress in the Americas, the Alcázar. After Diego left his post in 1523, the council remained in control and continued to expand the city of Santo Domingo, including building a university in 1538. By this time, all of the enslaved people there were Africans, and they built the growing city.

An Island Adrift

Spain continued to explore and take over land in Central and South America, and eventually the Spanish conquerors' attention and resources moved on to the new colonies. This gave other groups the chance to take advantage of the island's resources. In 1586, English explorer Sir Francis Drake took hold of Santo Domingo and held it for ransom until Spain paid him to give it back. Hispaniola was also a favorite spot for pirates and illegal traders, including the infamous Blackbeard. There was little government control or law enforcement, and the island's many secluded harbors were excellent spots to hide ships. By the end of the 1500s, the western end of the island had been almost entirely deserted by the Spanish. Those who remained were under self-rule.

As Spain lost its grip on Hispaniola, French troops occupied the western end of the island and began to move eastward. The two countries fought over the land until the Treaty of Ryswick in 1697, but the French continued to occupy the western territory, which they named Saint-Domingue. The French side of Hispaniola grew far more prosperous than the Spanish side.

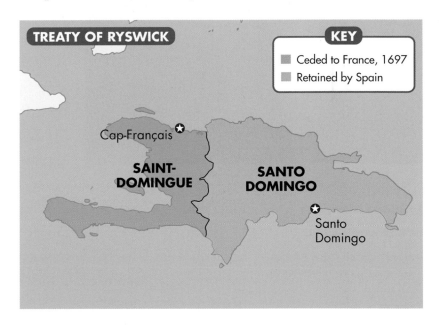

Toussaint Louverture helped lead Haiti to independence from France.

Fighting for Control

Both the French and the Spanish on Hispaniola bought enslaved people, bringing thousands to the island in the late 1700s. During this time, an antislavery movement was brewing in Saint-Domingue. In August 1791, the black slaves rose up against their oppressors in what is known as the Haitian Revolution. The rebels quickly took over the entire island.

In the coming years, Haitian, French, and British armies competed for control of the island. Eventually, the Haitians triumphed in the western part of the island. On the eastern side of the island, the Spanish-speaking colonists and the British gained control, and in 1809 they reunited the colony with Spain. This did not last long, however. In 1821, the colony declared independence from Spain, calling itself Spanish Haiti.

Soon, however, Haitian troops from the west invaded Spanish Haiti. In 1822, they gained control, and the island was once again reunited. Under Haitian rule, slavery was abolished in the region.

Seeds of Independence

Many Dominicans resented Haitian control of their country. In 1838, Juan Pablo Duarte, the son of a wealthy Dominican family, founded a secret society dedicated to Haitian rule. After several years, the revolutionaries achieved victory in Santo Domingo in 1844. They declared independence, and the Dominican Republic was born.

The first president was Pedro Santana, an early supporter of the revolution. He resigned in 1848 after the first constitution was adopted. He took charge of the military, wanting to prevent another Haitian takeover. Buenaventura Báez followed Santana as president, but the two leaders competed for control. By 1861, the presidency had switched between them frequently, and the nation was divided. In hopes of keeping Haiti from taking advantage of the weakened country, Santana asked Queen Isabela II of Spain for support.

The Spanish troops arrived, but with their help came a price. The young nation became a Spanish colony once again, at the mercy of foreign rule and subjected to high taxes. But the Spanish soldiers soon fell victim to yellow fever, and a new rebellion called the War for the Restoration began. In 1865 the Spanish withdrew and the Dominican Republic was independent once more.

The Young Republic

Unfortunately, self-rule continued to be difficult for the young nation. Over the next seventeen years, the presidency changed hands twelve times. Different regions of the country fought each other, and there was constant unrest.

In 1882, Ulises Heureaux became president. During his time in office, he managed to build roads and railways and install communications systems like the telegraph. Unfortunately, he also became a tyrannical leader and managed the nation's finances poorly, sending the country into debt. He was assassinated in 1899.

U.S. Involvement

Foreign countries that had loaned money to the Dominican government began to get nervous that the debt would not be repaid. The United States was especially concerned about the political situation in the Caribbean. After a victory in the Spanish-American War in 1898, the United States had gained control of many territories in the Caribbean. The Americans worried that instability in the Dominican Republic would bring European troops back to the region.

U.S. president Theodore Roosevelt also wanted to complete the Panama Canal across the narrowest part of Central America, enabling ships to travel between the Atlantic and the Pacific Oceans without sailing all the way around South America. Roosevelt wanted to ensure that no political unrest might hinder the project or access to the canal once it was complete.

In 1905, a deal was made between the United States and the Dominican Republic. The United States took responsibility of repaying the Dominican debt. In return, American troops took control of all Dominican customs houses, where taxes on imports are collected. The Americans would put 55

percent of the customs duties toward paying off Dominican debt and give the remaining 45 percent to the Dominican government. The previous customs system had been so corrupt that the new income from less than half of the taxes was far more than the government was making before.

The economy began to improve, but the political situation continued to get worse. After a decade of rebellions, assassinations, and growing unrest, the U.S. government stepped in. In 1916, U.S. troops began an eight-year occupation. Under

U.S. Marine patrol boats gather on the Ozama River in Santo Domingo in 1919. The United States occupied the Dominican Republic for eight years in the early twentieth century.

Poet and Politician

Fabio Fiallo was a Dominican journalist, poet, teacher, and political activist. He founded three newspapers and was a popular poet.

Fiallo worked as a diplomat, serving in New York, Cuba, and Germany, before being elected governor of Santo Domingo in 1913. He was strongly opposed to the U.S. occupation and was one of the first Dominicans to protest the occupation among the international community. His articles opposing U.S. intervention in the Dominican Republic led to his being imprisoned. He was later exiled to Cuba, where he died in 1942.

In 1977, the Dominican government brought Fiallo's remains back to his homeland, where they were buried in the National Pantheon in Santo Domingo, a place of honor for Dominican patriots.

In the Dominican Republic, Fabio Fiallo was known as "the poet of love."

the occupation, new roads, schools, and hospitals were built. Laws were changed giving U.S. sugar companies greater power in the country.

Many Dominicans were opposed to the occupation. Some U.S. soldiers treated Dominicans badly, and censorship was imposed to discourage opposition. Dominicans who spoke out against the new policies were imprisoned, and some were executed. The occupation of the Dominican Republic was unpopular in the U.S. as well, and by 1924 the troops had left the island.

The Trujillo Years

In 1918, a young man named Rafael Trujillo joined the Dominican army. By 1927, he had worked his way up the ranks to become the commander of the national army. In 1930, Trujillo rigged a coup and took control of the government. He would remain in power as dictator until 1961. His three-decade regime would prove to be extraordinarily cruel and repressive.

Trujillo did not try to hide his appetite for wealth and power. In 1936, he changed the name of Santo Domingo to Trujillo (Trujillo City) after himself. The nation's highest mountain was renamed Trujillo Peak. He dominated the Church and took over ownership of many businesses. The country was his.

During the Trujillo years, the Dominican economy continued to grow, and foreign debt was finally eliminated. The nation's infrastructure expanded with new roads, railways, seaports, and airports, which in turn helped industry thrive. Mining, farming, and livestock production increased, and a middle class began to develop. Education and living standards improved, and the government established policies that helped the poor. On paper, the Dominican Republic was a successful society.

But the reality was much darker. Although there were elections periodically, Trujillo made sure that there was no real competition to his power. He put trusted followers in office as president, and then he pulled the strings of these puppet presidents. The real government was Trujillo, who was an absolute dictator, and he extinguished any threats that came along. His loyal army was careful to ensure that opponents disappeared quickly. Those who spoke out openly against him were jailed or killed. Trujillo's most horrible act as dictator was the slaughter in 1937 of about fifteen thousand Haitians who lived just over the border in the Dominican Republic.

Finally, the rest of the world realized what was happening in the Dominican Republic. In 1960, Trujillo attempted to have the president of Venezuela assassinated after he

As dictator of the Dominican Republic, Rafael Trujillo (center) acquired great wealth. He became the nation's largest landholder and dominated the sugar, tobacco, lumber, dairy, and meat industries.

had criticized the dictator's harsh rule. The Organization of American States (OAS)—an organization of countries in the Western Hemisphere—ousted the Dominican Republic, and the United States cut ties with the Dominican government. The Catholic Church excommunicated Trujillo, meaning he was barred from taking part in many rituals. On May 30, 1961, Dominican army leaders assassinated Rafael Trujillo with the support of the U.S. Central Intelligence Agency.

Dominicans attend a vigil on the Dominican-Haitian border commemorating the anniversary of the massacre of thousands of Haitians in 1937.

A New Era Begins

When Trujillo was killed, his political puppet Joaquín Balaguer held the office of president. Balaguer immediately renounced Trujillo and began to change policies. He also exiled the Trujillo family after they attempted to regain power. The people still did not trust that Balaguer would be different from his former boss, and he was ousted in 1962.

In 1961, Dominicans filled the streets of Santo Domingo, protesting Joaquín Balaguer's government.

The first real free election since 1924 was held on December 20, 1962. Juan Bosch of the Dominican Revolutionary Party (PRD) was the winner, and as president he immediately worked with other officials to draft a new constitution. The Constitution of 1963 restored civil rights to the Dominican people, gave civilians control over the military, and officially separated church and state. The nation was accepted back into the OAS, and international relationships were repaired. Despite these promising changes, Bosch was forced from office by the military within a year. The military remained in power until a democratic revolt broke out in 1965.

U.S. Forces Return

As the revolt grew, officials in the United States became concerned that the Dominican Republic might be on the road to communist revolution. Communism is an economic system in which the government controls the economy and owns most businesses. At the time, the United States was in the midst of the Cold War, a global power struggle with the communist Soviet Union, a large country that has since broken up to become Russia and many neighboring nations. Cuba, another Caribbean nation, had recently become communist, and the United States did not want a second communist nation nearby. In addition, in the years after Trujillo's death, U.S. companies had poured money into real estate in the Dominican Republic. The country's political upheavals were causing problems for the wealthy U.S.

U.S. troops move through Santo Domingo in 1965. More than forty thousand American troops were involved in the invasion.

corporations that wanted to develop there. So to both protect U.S. corporate interest and prevent the spread of communism, in 1965, U.S. president Lyndon B. Johnson sent troops to the Dominican Republic to put down the revolt and occupy the country once again.

The following year, new elections were held, and U.S. forces were withdrawn. Joaquín Balaguer, running as a moderate who would restore order to the country, won the election for president. He served twelve years in office, and during that time he made many reforms. One important change was that he began appointing members of opposing political parties to government positions, something that had never been done before. But, like Trujillo, he was a repressive leader, limiting civil liberties. Many people left the Dominican Republic for the United States, particularly New York City, during this era.

More Recent Times

In the 1978 elections, the PRD candidate Antonio Guzmán Fernández, with the support of the United States, defeated Balaguer to win the presidency. In 1982, another PRD candidate, Salvador Jorge Blanco, became president. Blanco succeeded in reducing inflation and tried to improve the system of free elections. But faced with falling sugar prices and other economic difficulties, he lost the 1986 elections to Joaquín Balaguer, who remained in power until 1996.

Balaguer was forced to step down when it became clear that he had rigged the most recent elections in 1994 against José Francisco Peña Gómez, the longtime leader of the PRD.

A special election was held following the resignation, and a progressive named Leonel Fernández won. Fernández's policies were focused on strengthening foreign relations and increasing trade, and during his time in office the economy grew quickly. In 2000, Hipólito Mejía became president, but during his time in office the economy collapsed, and he lost his reelection bid.

Leonel Fernández returned to office. He and his successor, Danilo Medina, both benefited from the country's booming economy. A subway system opened in Santo Domingo in 2009, and tourism, construction, and mining have all expanded. In recent years, the Dominican Republic has had one of the fastest-growing economies in the Western Hemisphere.

Workers construct the nation's first subway system in Santo Domingo. The project employed more than four thousand workers.

CHAPTER 5

Democracy in Action

SINCE THE DEATH OF DICTATOR RAFAEL TRUJILLO, the Dominican Republic has struggled to establish a fair election system. As the system improves, Dominicans continue to push for more control over their own government.

The country has several political parties that have representatives in office. The Dominican Liberation Party (PLD) and the Modern Revolutionary Party (PRM) are the most powerful, although the Social Christian Reformist Party (PRSC) and the Dominican Revolutionary Party (PRD) also have significant influence. In addition, there are more than a dozen other smaller parties.

The Constitution

The most recent constitution of the Dominican Republic was adopted in 2010. This document outlines the structure of the

Opposite: **Members of the Presidential Guard take part in a ceremony honoring veterans.**

A Look at the Dominican Flag

The flag of the Dominican Republic shows four rectangles, two red and two blue, with a white cross separating them. Blue represents liberty. Red stands for the blood of the heroes who died preserving liberty. The white cross is a symbol of salvation.

In the center of the cross is the nation's coat of arms, which includes a shield, a symbol of strength, with six spears representing protection. The coat of arms is decorated in the national colors and bears images of the Bible, a gold cross, a laurel branch, and a palm frond. A blue banner above the shield declares the national motto, "Dios, Patria, Libertad" (God,

The flag of the Dominican Republic was adopted in 1844 and later modified.

Home, Liberty). A red banner below holds the nation's name, Republica Dominicana.

government. It also sets limits on presidential power, determines election policies, addresses civil rights of citizens, and sets the political subdivisions of the country and their powers and responsibility. The basic government structure is similar to that of the United States.

Executive Branch

The executive branch of government includes the president, the vice president, and the cabinet. The president is the head of government, the head of state, and the commander in chief of the country's armed forces.

The president is elected by the people to a four-year term. He or she can serve two terms. The vice president is elected with the president. Members of the cabinet are nominated directly by the president and are responsible for overseeing specific areas of policy.

National Government of the Dominican Republic

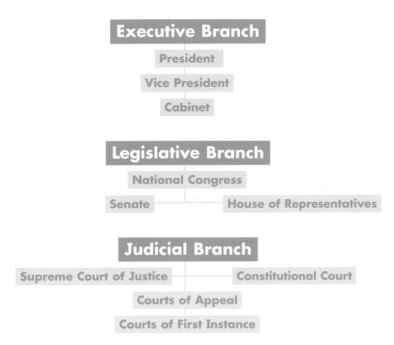

Executive Branch
President
Vice President
Cabinet

Legislative Branch
National Congress
Senate — House of Representatives

Judicial Branch
Supreme Court of Justice — Constitutional Court
Courts of Appeal
Courts of First Instance

Legislative Branch

The legislative branch is known as the National Congress. It is made up of two parts, the Senate and the House of Representatives. This branch of government is responsible for keeping the president's power in check—most importantly to prevent another dictatorship. It is also responsible for passing laws. Representatives from most major political parties usually serve in this branch, although the PRD and PRM hold most of the seats and the smaller parties have low representation.

The National Palace houses the offices of the executive branch. It was built in the 1940s on the orders of Rafael Trujillo.

The Senate has thirty-two seats, one person elected from each province. The House of Representatives has approximately 190 seats, which are determined by proportional representation, meaning that the more citizens a region has, the more representatives it will have in the House. Each seat represents around fifty thousand people, so the number of representatives changes as the population grows. The House of Representatives also includes seven seats elected by Dominicans living abroad. Two of these seats are designated for people living in the Caribbean, in Latin America, and in Miami, Florida; three are for people living elsewhere in the

United States or Canada; and two are for people in Europe. Both Senate and House terms are four years.

Judicial Branch

The judicial branch of government consists of the court system. The Supreme Court of Justice has at least sixteen judges who serve seven-year terms. Each judge is appointed by the National Council of the Judiciary, which includes the Supreme Court President, the leaders of both legislative houses, and the president. The 2010 constitution added a second high court, the Constitutional Court. Its purpose is to rule

Danilo Medina was elected president in 2012. The nation's economy grew during his time in office, and he was easily reelected four years later.

The National Anthem

The official anthem of the Dominican Republic is called simply "Himno Nacional" (National Anthem). The lyrics were written by Emilio Prud'Homme, and the music was composed by José Reyes. The anthem was adopted in 1897. The original song is quite long, but usually only the shorter version below is performed.

Spanish lyrics	English translation
Quisqueyanos valientes alcemos	Brave men of Quisqueya,
Nuestro canto con viva emoción,	Let us sing with strong feeling
Y del mundo a la faz ostentemos	And let us show to the world
Nuestro invicto glorioso pendón.	Our invincible, glorious banner.
¡Salve! el pueblo que, intrépido y fuerte.	Hail, O people who, strong and intrepid,
A la guerra a morir se lanzó,	Launched into war and went to death!
Cuando en bélico reto de muerte	Under a warlike menace of death,
Sus cadenas de esclavo rompió.	You broke your chains of slavery.
Ningún pueblo ser libre merece	No country deserves to be free
Si es esclavo, indolente y servil,	If it is an indolent and servile slave,
Si en su pecho la llama no crece	If the call does not grow loud within it,
Que templó el heroismo viril.	Tempered by a virile heroism.
Mas Quisqueya la indómita y brava	But the brave and indomitable Quisqueya
Siempre altiva la frente alzará;	Will always hold its head high,
Que si fuere mil veces esclava	For if it were a thousand times enslaved,
Otras tantas ser libre sabrá.	It would a thousand times regain freedom.

on issues specific to the constitution. It is made up of thirteen judges who serve nine-year terms.

The lower courts include many divisions, each depending on the type of case. This includes Courts of Appeal, Courts of First Instance, and specialized courts.

Local Government

The Dominican Republic is divided into thirty-one provinces, which are laid out in the constitution. Each province has a governor who is appointed by the president. Each province elects one member of the senate and a proportional number of representatives in the house.

The National District is also represented in the National Congress, although it is not considered a province. Like Washington, D.C., the National District contains only one municipality, the capital city of Santo Domingo. It does not have a governor.

Provinces are divided into municipal districts, similar to the way U.S. states are divided into counties. Leaders of these districts are elected by residents in a popular vote, as are leaders of towns and cities.

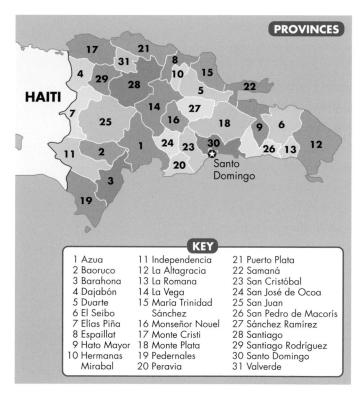

PROVINCES

HAITI

Santo Domingo

KEY

1 Azua	11 Independencia	21 Puerto Plata
2 Baoruco	12 La Altagracia	22 Samaná
3 Barahona	13 La Romana	23 San Cristóbal
4 Dajabón	14 La Vega	24 San José de Ocoa
5 Duarte	15 María Trinidad	25 San Juan
6 El Seibo	Sánchez	26 San Pedro de Macorís
7 Elías Piña	16 Monseñor Nouel	27 Sánchez Ramírez
8 Espaillat	17 Monte Cristi	28 Santiago
9 Hato Mayor	18 Monte Plata	29 Santiago Rodríguez
10 Hermanas	19 Pedernales	30 Santo Domingo
Mirabal	20 Peravia	31 Valverde

A Look at the Capital

The capital city of Santo Domingo has a population of more than 2.9 million, making it the largest city in the Dominican Republic and all of the Caribbean. The city was originally founded in 1496 by Bartholomew Columbus on the east bank of the Ozama River, but it was moved to the west bank in 1502 after a hurricane destroyed the first city. It is the oldest continuously inhabited city established by Europeans in the Americas.

Santo Domingo is not only the center of the Dominican government but also the heart of the nation's economy. It is the nation's financial and commercial capital as well as a major industrial center and transportation hub.

Santo Domingo also has a growing tourist industry. Many people come to explore the city's historic district or relax on the nearby beaches. The city is also home to a lively performing arts and social scene.

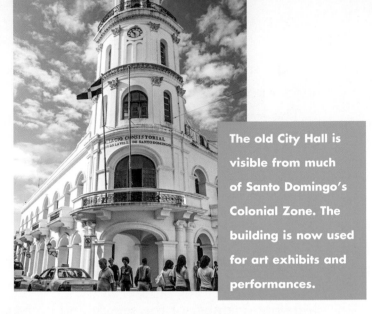

The old City Hall is visible from much of Santo Domingo's Colonial Zone. The building is now used for art exhibits and performances.

SANTO DOMINGO

0   0.25 MI
0   0.25 KM

Enriquillo Park

to U.S. embassy

Ozama River

Palace of Diego Columbus
Plaza de la Hispanidad

National Pantheon

National Palace

Columbus Park

House of Bastidas

Calle Las Damas

Ozama Fortress

Cathedral of Santa María la Menor

Independence Park

COLONIAL ZONE

to Autonomous University of Santo Domingo

Eugenio Maria de Hostos Park

San Souci Lighthouse Park

Voting

Dominican citizens age eighteen and over, as well as anyone who is legally married no matter their age, have the right to vote in local and nationwide elections. However, members of the national police, members of the armed forces, and prisoners are not allowed to vote.

In recent times, citizens have been turning out to vote in greater numbers. In the past, many chose not to vote because they thought that their ballot would not be secret and they might be punished, which happened during the time of Rafael Trujillo's dictatorship. Some people have also been skeptical of voting because of the nation's history of rigged elections and suspicious ballot counts.

A Dominican woman casts her ballot during a presidential election. In 2016, about 70 percent of registered voters went to the polls.

CHAPTER 6

The Dominican Economy

THE DOMINICAN REPUBLIC HAS ONE OF THE FAST-est-growing economies in the Americas. For many years, the Dominican Republic's economy was dependent upon agriculture. The most valuable cash crop was sugarcane, followed by tobacco. Over recent decades, however, services such as tourism, finance, and trade have become more important.

Remittances are also an important part of the economy. This is money sent home by people who have left the country. It is common for young people to move to the United States or other countries to work. Even if they are making minimum wage in the United States, they are earning far more than they would if they had remained in the Dominican Republic. In 2016, Dominicans living abroad sent more than $5 billion home to their families.

Opposite: **A Dominican truck is piled high with bananas. The nation's banana industry has changed in recent years as the country has become the world's leading producer of organic bananas.**

Dominican teachers lead an exercise class for tourists at a resort on the east coast.

Services

The service sector is central to the Dominican economy. Approximately two-thirds of the workforce is employed in a service job. Service sector jobs include anything where people do not grow, make, or mine a product. These jobs include teachers, bankers, doctors, bus drivers, store clerks, and waiters.

Tourism is a growing part of the Dominican economy. In 2017, more than six million tourists vacationed in the Dominican Republic, making it the most visited country in the Caribbean. Most tourists stay at large beach resorts and spend most of their time there. Port cities like Puerto Plata and Santo Domingo are also popular stops for cruise ships, which bring in day tourists.

Most of the Dominican Republic's resorts are owned by large foreign companies. Although these resorts provide jobs in housekeeping, food service, maintenance, and other guest services, many tourists spend little money outside the resorts. They do not contribute to smaller, Dominican-owned businesses. In addition, many of the resorts, built right along the coast, are harmful to the environment. Native trees and plants that hold the soil in place are removed to build the resorts, making erosion a greater problem. Sometimes scarce water is also diverted to tourist areas from other places where it is needed.

Agriculture

Once dominant in the Dominican economy, today agriculture employs only about 14 percent of the workforce. Some farms are operated by families or small groups, and others are large commercial farms similar to the plantations of the past. The large farms are often owned by foreign investors and grow cash crops such as sugarcane, tobacco, cotton, and rice. Coffee, cocoa beans, rice, and bananas are also exported, as well as fruits and vegetables like tomatoes that are sold during the winter months to places around the world where they are out of season.

Smaller farms grow a large variety of crops, including staples like rice, corn, beans, and potatoes. Fruits and vegetables such as lettuce, cabbage,

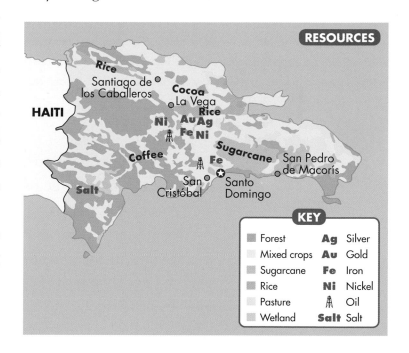

RESOURCES

Rice
Santiago de los Caballeros
Cocoa
La Vega
HAITI
Ni
Rice
Au Ag
Fe Ni
Coffee
Fe
Sugarcane
San Pedro de Macorís
San Cristóbal
Santo Domingo
Salt

KEY

■ Forest	**Ag**	Silver
■ Mixed crops	**Au**	Gold
■ Sugarcane	**Fe**	Iron
■ Rice	**Ni**	Nickel
■ Pasture	⚒	Oil
■ Wetland	**Salt**	Salt

After cutting the sugarcane, workers pile it into large carts.

In the Sugarcane Fields

Many of the laborers on the large plantations are Haitian migrants. On sugarcane plantations, Haitian workers live in shacks without running water or electricity. Many work in the hot fields twelve hours a day, even though the legal limit is ten hours. Workers are paid by the ton of cut sugarcane. But a long day's work earns them only about the equivalent of $11. The Haitian workers lack many medical and social benefits. Many are forced to work into old age, but as they get older, they cannot cut as much cane, so they earn less. For many, it is a hard life with no relief.

avocados, guava, passion fruit, mangoes, and coconuts are grown year-round. Some of these crops are exported and some are consumed at home.

Dominican farmers also raise livestock, almost all of which is consumed in the Dominican Republic. People in rural areas tend to have their own small farms to feed their families. Many raise livestock including goats for dairy products, chickens for meat and eggs, and pigs. Some also raise sheep for both meat and wool. The country also has some large farms that raise pigs and chickens for sale, and cattle farms provide both dairy and beef.

Mining

The history of commercial mining in the Dominican Republic dates back to the early days of European colonization. Gold mining is still a major industry, and the mines at Pueblo Viejo in the central part of the country are some of the largest in the world. Ferronickel mining (iron ore and nickel) is also a major industry. Other resources mined in the Dominican Republic include silver, copper, and bauxite.

A light blue stone called larimar is found only in the Dominican Republic. This beautiful stone is often used in

Larimar is a blue variety of a mineral called pectolite. While pectolite is common, larimar is found only in the Dominican Republic.

jewelry. Amber, although not actually a gemstone, is also mined throughout the island. Combined, precious metals and gemstones make up approximately 22 percent of Dominican exports, and finished jewelry accounts for another 5 percent.

What the Nation Grows, Makes, and Mines

Agriculture (2016)

Sugarcane	4,717,490 metric tons
Bananas	1,079,781 metric tons
Chickens	171,883,000 head

Manufacturing (2016, value of exports)

Medical instruments	$1.33 billion
Tobacco products	$774 million
Machines	$759 million

Mining (2016, value of exports)

Gold	$ 1.68 billion
Copper	$45.9 million
Silver	$28.5 million

Manufacturing and Free Trade Zones

The manufacturing industry includes processing crops and natural resources. Tobacco is turned into cigars. Sugarcane and cocoa beans are processed before they are exported. Metals and other mining products are also usually processed locally before being shipped out of the country.

Most of the rest of the manufacturing in the Dominican Republic happens in free trade zones. In these areas foreign companies are allowed to set up factories and export goods without paying import taxes on the raw materials they bring in or export taxes on the finished products. They also pay a very low income tax rate or avoid paying them altogether, depending on their agreement. At one time, factories in the free trade zone did not have to pay a minimum wage to

The Dominican Republic is one of the leading cigar-producing countries. Cigars are made by hand. The cigar maker first rolls the tobacco leaves and then puts on a label.

Trade Partners (2017)	
Top Export Destinations	
United States	53%
Haiti	10%
Canada	9%
India	7%
Switzerland	3%
Top Import Sources	
United States	45%
China	13%
Mexico	5%
Brazil	3%
Spain	3%

workers. This has changed as human rights activists have put pressure on the companies, and now the Dominican government requires that all workers in free trade zones be paid a minimum of about $165 per month. This is still far less than the companies would have to pay in their home countries such as the United States, saving them even more money. The Dominican government considers free trade zones good for the economy because they provide some jobs, but most of the profits flow out of the country.

Some of the free trade zone companies manufacture textiles like T-shirts and jeans. Other factories produce

Many Dominican exports are packed into huge containers to be shipped around the world.

The Dominican Peso

The official currency in the Dominican Republic is called the Dominican peso. Paper currency is printed in denominations of 5, 10, 20, 50, 500, and 1,000 pesos. Coins are available in denominations of 1, 5, 10, and 25 pesos. The colorful bills depict important people and monuments from Dominican history. For example, the 200-peso bill depicts the Mirabel sisters, who were murdered for their efforts opposing the dictatorship of Rafael Trujillo. In 2018, 1 Dominican peso equaled 2¢, and 50 Dominican pesos equaled $1.

Dominican banknotes are colorful. The 100-peso bill is orange and green.

electronics, medical supplies, and toys. More recently, other types of industries have begun taking advantage of free trade zones. These include call centers, advertising agencies, telemarketing, and travel agencies.

Trade

The Dominican Republic imports goods such as cell phones, gasoline, cars, plastic products, chemicals, and medications. The United States is the country's biggest trade partner, receiving more than half of Dominican exports and providing about 45 percent of goods imported into the Dominican Republic. Neighboring Haiti purchases about 10 percent of Dominican exports, but is not a significant source of goods.

CHAPTER 7

Meet the Dominicans

I N 2018, AN ESTIMATED 10,914,696 PEOPLE LIVED IN the Dominican Republic. Roughly four out of five live in urban areas, most in the cities of Santo Domingo and Santiago de los Caballeros. The nation has a young population, with about 45 percent under the age of twenty-five. Only 16 percent of Dominicans are over fifty-five.

Dominican Society

Social classes are distinct in the Dominican Republic. They are related both to people's economic level and to the color of their skin. Families in the wealthy and powerful upper class are usually descendants of the early Spanish settlers and have light skin.

Families in the lowest economic and social classes are descended from slaves brought from Africa or Haitians from

Opposite: **Dominican girls at a festival in Santo Domingo. About one in three Dominicans lives in the Santo Domingo area.**

Population of Major Cities

Santo Domingo	2,908,607
Santiago de los Caballeros	553,091
La Vega	210,736
San Cristóbal	209,165
San Pedro de Macorís	205,911

the other side of the island of Hispaniola. They tend to have darker skin. The vast majority of Dominicans are of mixed background, with both African and European ancestors. There are also small numbers of people of Asian ancestry, including people of Japanese, Chinese, Lebanese, and Syrian descent.

In recent times, a middle class has grown in Dominican society. Today, about one-third of Dominicans are middle class. They are employed as teachers and office workers, and in the government and the military. Some own shops and small businesses. Most middle-class Dominicans live in Santo Domingo, but some reside in other cities.

The nation's largest socioeconomic group is the lower class, which accounts for about half the population. Most of the people who live in rural areas struggle to make a living on small farms or work as migrant laborers. Many families do not make enough to meet their needs. Many Dominicans move to the city in search of work, but there they find little affordable housing, so they are forced to live in run-down shacks without running water or electricity.

POPULATION

KEY

Persons per square mile	Persons per square kilometer
more than 520	more than 200
260–520	100–200
130–260	50–100
65–130	25–50
26–65	10–25
3–26	1–10
fewer than 3	fewer than 1

Many Dominicans of Haitian descent live in bateyes, settlements established for workers on sugarcane plantations.

The Color Divide

Dominicans often describe people as belonging to one of four racial categories. *Blanco* refers to those who are of entirely European ancestry, usually the upper class. *Indio claro* and *indio oscuro* refer to people who are of mixed European and African ancestry. Those described as indio blanco have lighter skin than those who are indio oscuro. *Negro,* the Spanish word for "black," is used for people of pure African ancestry and usually refers to people of Haitian descent.

Most Dominicans are of mixed African and European background. Few have Taíno ancestors. But because many Dominicans are hostile toward Haitians, some Dominicans do not want to acknowledge their own African roots. As a result, the term *indio*, referring to indigenous people, is used, promoting the myth that they are of Taíno rather than African descent.

The dictator Rafael Trujillo was of mixed descent. He promoted this myth and claimed that his skin color came from Taíno roots. Because Trujillo did not want to be considered black, he used makeup to make his skin look lighter. He aroused hatred toward Haitians by promoting racist propaganda against them. Even today, Haitians and other black people living in the Dominican Republic are treated poorly.

A woman holds a sign proclaiming "Soy dominicano," "I am Dominican," at a protest of the Constitutional Court's ruling that left Haitian Dominicans stateless.

New Rules for Haitians

For much of history, a child of any background who was born in the Dominican Republic was considered a citizen, just as any child born in the United States is a U.S. citizen. But in 2013, the Dominican Constitutional Court ruled that only people born in the Dominican Republic to Dominican parents or legal residents are citizens. According to the court, this judgment applied to anyone born in the Dominican Republic between 1929 and 2010. Suddenly, hundreds of thousands of people who had been born in the Dominican Republic to Haitian migrants were no longer considered citizens. Even if they had lived their entire lives in the Dominican Republic, had Dominican passports and voter ID cards, they were now stateless, citizens of no country.

The ruling created an international outcry. In response to the uproar, in 2014 the Dominican government created a process enabling people to reclaim their Dominican citizenship. But the process was complicated. The documents required were difficult if not impossible for many people to get. By the time the deadline for this process passed, only a few thousand people had reclaimed their citizenship. The others remain in limbo, without rights, fearful of being deported to a country where they have never been.

Health

In the Dominican Republic, people do not have equal access to health care. Doctors and hospitals are typically only available in major cities. In addition, medical care is expensive, and many people suffer from lack of clean water and poor nutrition. Consequently, twenty-one out of every one thousand babies die before they reach the age of one. By contrast, four babies out of every one thousand born in the United States die before age one.

Ethnic Background (2014 est.)	
Mixed	70.4%
Black	15.8%
White	13.5%
Other	0.3%

Looking for Opportunities

Many Dominicans leave their home country every year in hopes of finding better jobs and greater opportunities. Most

Some Dominicans live in shacks made of scraps of metal and wood.

are bound for the United States, but many also live in Italy, Spain, Venezuela, Chile, Argentina, Dubai, and many other places around the world. Those working abroad send money, known as remittances, home to help their families.

Today, nearly two million people of Dominican descent live in the United States. About 55 percent are immigrants. The others had parents, grandparents, or more remote ancestors who arrived in the United States from the Dominican Republic. The first big wave of Dominican immigrants to the United States arrived in the 1960s, and large numbers of Dominicans continued to immigrate throughout the rest of the twentieth century.

Members of a traditional dance troupe take part in the Dominican Day parade in New York City. Dominicans are now the largest Latino group in the city.

About three-fourths of those who immigrate to the United States live in the New York, Boston, or Miami metropolitan areas. Dominicans who settle in these places join thriving communities. In New York, more than half a million people celebrate Dominican Day with a gala parade each August. Similar parades are held in Boston and in Paterson, New Jersey.

Dominican students take a field trip to the Colonial Zone in Santo Domingo. The school year in the Dominican Republic is similar to that in the United States, with a summer break that lasts about two months.

Education

According to Dominican law, children are supposed to attend school for at least seven years. Most Dominican children begin school, but only about three-quarters of them complete all seven grades. Many drop out because their families need them to work or care for younger brothers and sisters while their parents work.

After reaching the sixth grade, students are divided into two tracks for high school. Students on the academic track are those

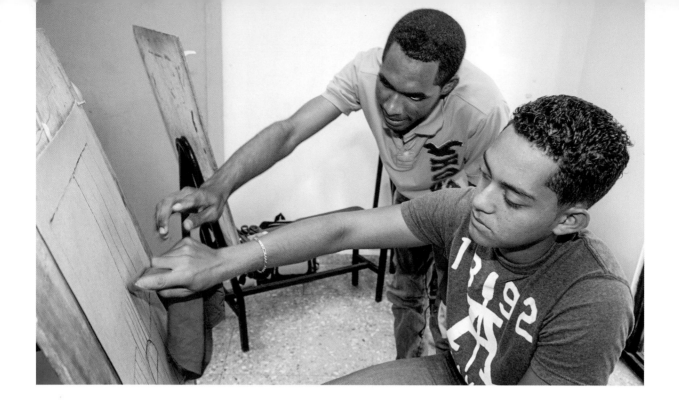

A teacher advises a student at an art school in Santo Domingo.

planning to go to college. Students on the technical track are training for jobs in business, agriculture, or industry. About 67 percent of girls and 58 percent of boys attend high school.

Schools in the Dominican Republic face persistent problems. Teachers are paid little and are often poorly trained. Because of this, the quality of education is sometimes low. In recent years, the government has increased the education budget, setting aside money to build more schools and hire more teachers.

Children from wealthy families often go to private elementary school. Many are sent to Europe or the United States for high school and college.

The nation's major public university is the Autonomous University of Santo Domingo. Founded in 1538, it is the oldest institution of higher education in the Americas. Tuition at this university is free. Most Dominican universities are privately owned, and it is expensive for students to attend those colleges.

Language

When the Spanish colonized the island of Hispaniola, they brought their language with them. The Spanish spoken in the Dominican Republic today has been enriched by words from other languages. The Spanish adopted Taíno words for things that were unfamiliar to them. They used local terms for plants such as tobacco and cassava. The word *hurricane* comes from

A tobacco field in the Dominican Republic. The word *tobacco* comes in part from a Taíno word that referred to a roll of tobacco leaves.

the Taíno language. A word for farm, *conuco*, is from Taíno, as is the word *chin*, which means "a little bit."

Dominican Spanish also includes a few surviving words from Old Spanish, the form of Spanish spoken at the time when Europeans first arrived in the region. These include *tato* (good) and *mato* (tree).

Other languages spoken in the Dominican Republic include Haitian Creole, a mixed language with French, Spanish, and West African influences. It is spoken by some people of Haitian descent. Some people who trace their roots to Asia speak Japanese, Korean, or Arabic.

Chinese Dominicans attend a Chinese New Year celebration in Santo Domingo.

A sign in Spanish at a taxi stand on the Samaná Peninsula

Spanish, Dominican Style

Some of these Spanish phrases you may hear anywhere, but others are unique to the Dominican Republic.

Hola	Hello
Adiós	Good-bye
Buenos días	Good morning
Buenas noches	Good evening
¿Cómo se llama?	What is your name?
Me llamo Juan.	My name is John.
Por favor	Please
Gracias	Thank you
De nada	You're welcome
¿Qué lo qué?	What's up? (Dominican slang)
Vaina	Thing that is complicated or irritating (Dominican slang)
Jeva/Jevo	Girl/boy (Dominican slang)
Colmado	Convenience store (Dominican slang)

CHAPTER 8

Spiritual Traditions

T HE DOMINICAN CONSTITUTION GRANTS FREEDOM of religion to all citizens of the nation. More than two-thirds of the people in the country belong to the Roman Catholic Church. Another quarter are Protestant. Smaller numbers of people practice Islam, Judaism, and other religions. Traditional folk religions are also practiced freely.

Roman Catholicism

About 70 percent of Dominicans identify as Roman Catholic. The first Spaniards to arrive in the region brought this religion with them. The first Catholic mass in the Americas was held in 1494 near the settlement at La Isabela. The Cathedral of Santa María la Menor, the first cathedral in the Western Hemisphere, was completed in 1541. Throughout the colonial era, the Church had a great deal of power over the government.

Opposite: **A woman holds palm fronds as part of a Palm Sunday ceremony, a week before Easter. Palm Sunday commemorates the Christian story that says when Jesus entered Jerusalem people spread palm leaves in front of him.**

Religious Groups	
Roman Catholic	70%
Protestant	26%
No religion/atheist	3%
Other	1%

In 1954, dictator Rafael Trujillo signed a treaty called a concordat with the Vatican, the center of the Roman Catholic Church. He did this to control both the people and the Church. Because of his support for the Church, Catholic leaders were reluctant to speak out against his policies. Only near the end of his rule did the Church excommunicate him, or ban him from taking part in important Catholic rituals.

The concordat is still in effect today. Under this document, the Catholic Church enjoys special privileges that other religions do not have. Public funds are sometimes used to support

A Dominican bride in Santo Domingo. In the Dominican Republic, brides usually wear white.

the Church. The Catholic Church has input in textbooks used in public schools. In addition, marriages performed by Catholic priests are automatically registered with the government. People married in other religions must register their marriage with the government themselves to make it legal.

In general, Catholic priests in the Dominican Republic are both spiritual guides and social leaders. Many are involved with economic reform, working to end poverty. Many priests and nuns work directly with the people. Many nuns are teachers in schools and universities. Others run orphanages or work as nurses.

Catholic Traditions

For many Dominicans, religion is a major part of everyday life. Many people attend mass every week. A less common tradition is a large procession called a *rosario*, which is held in hopes of curing an illness or solving a problem like a drought.

Religious Holidays

Epiphany	January 6
Our Lady of Altagracia Day	January 21
Palm Sunday (Sunday prior to Easter)	March or April
Holy Thursday (Thursday prior to Easter)	March or April
Good Friday (Friday prior to Easter)	March or April
Easter Sunday	March or April
Corpus Christi	May or June
Our Lady of Mercy Day	September 24
Christmas Day	December 25

The Cathedral of Our Lady of Altagracia was completed in 1970.

The Importance of Shrines

Religious shrines and statues are important to many Dominicans, even those who are not practicing Roman Catholics. The most important shrine on the island is that of Our Lady of Altagracia at the cathedral in Higüey, a city in the eastern part of the Dominican Republic.

Our Lady of Altagracia is a version of the Virgin Mary. She is considered the nation's patron saint and protector, and many devout Catholics travel long distances to visit the shrine to pray. January 21 is the official day of celebration for Our Lady of Altagracia.

The leader of the rosario carries a large rosary (Catholic prayer beads) and an image of the Virgin Mary (Jesus's mother) or another saint. Musicians follow the procession, playing guitars, flutes, or other instruments. Behind them walk the Catholic faithful. It is believed that all of the members of the procession must complete the travel back to the starting point in order for the prayers to be answered.

As the religious parade passes from town to town, the group stops at stations, also called rosarios. These are groups of crosses that are erected in rural areas as a symbol of welcome to travelers and to serve as the meeting places for the processions.

Religious sites and statues are important symbols of faith for many Dominicans. Not all the shrines and statues are in public places. Almost every home has a shrine. Wealthier homes may have a large space with a statue of Mary decorated with flowers and surrounded by candles and religious objects. Poorer households may have only a small picture or figure, but these shrines are just as important.

Men dressed as Roman soldiers take part in a Good Friday procession in Santo Domingo. Good Friday is the day that Christians believe Jesus was crucified by the Romans.

Protestants

About one-quarter of Dominicans identify as Protestant Christians. This percentage is growing as many Catholics have converted. Major Protestant faiths in the country include the Dominican Evangelical Church, the Free Methodist Church, Seventh-Day Adventists, and the Assembly of God. In recent times, the numbers of Jehovah's Witnesses and members of the Church of Jesus Christ of Latter-day Saints, known as Mormons, have been increasing.

Dominicans worship at an Evangelical church near Barahona.

Other World Religions

During World War II, when Jewish people in Germany and other European countries were being persecuted, Rafael Trujillo opened his country to the refugees. The small town of Sosúa was established by a group of Jewish refugees, and a small number of the descendants of these refugees still live there. Santo Domingo has two synagogues, Jewish houses of worship, which serve a small Jewish population.

The Dominican Republic also has small populations of people who practice Islam, brought by immigrants from countries such as Syria, and Buddhism, brought by Japanese immigrants in the 1960s.

Muslims in Santo Domingo gather during Eid al-Fitr, the feast that celebrates the end of the holy month of Ramadan. Throughout Ramadan, Muslims fast during daylight hours.

Superstitions

In addition to official religious beliefs, some Dominicans also take superstitions to heart. Called *oraciones*, these "rules" tell people how to avoid bad luck and how to prevent unwanted ills. Have you heard of any of these before?

- It is bad luck if a wedding guest wears black.
- If an unmarried woman agrees to be a godmother, she will never marry.
- If an unmarried woman is a bridesmaid three times, she will never marry.
- If a couple weds in November, the marriage will not last.
- Opening an umbrella in the house invites bad luck.
- If a man sleeps with his feet pointed toward the front of the house, he will die.
- An image of a saint over the front door will keep evil from entering the house.

Folk Traditions

Many Dominicans, especially those in rural areas, combine Roman Catholicism with spiritual and healing traditions that have been passed down through generations. This is known as traditional folk religion. It is common for devout Catholics to consult a folk healer called a *curandero* for spiritual advice and help. The healer performs an *ensalmo*, a chant, which is said to enable him or her to communicate with saints in order to help people.

Some Dominicans also visit a *brujo*, who uses herbs and other plants for healing. Brujos are also believed to have the power to get rid of evil spirits.

Vodou

The rich ethnic mix in the Caribbean helped form a unique religion called Vodou. The word *vodou* means "god," "spirit," or "sacred object." It is a mixture of traditional African tribal beliefs, Taíno religions, and Roman Catholicism. Its basic structure includes one supreme being and many lesser spirits.

According to Vodou beliefs, each individual is watched by a spirit that rewards with wealth and punishes with illness.

A Vodou shrine in the Dominican Republic mixes Christian and non-Christian elements.

These spirits are considered family gods who are the souls of dead ancestors. They must be remembered regularly with elaborate memorials so they will continue to protect the living. Nature gods oversee the weather and other aspects of the natural world and are worshipped in seasonal celebrations.

Both men and women can be Vodou spiritual leaders. Male priests are called *hungans*, and females are called *mambos*. They provide guidance and perform a ritual that banishes *loas*, gods

During the week before Easter, some Dominicans take part in *gagá* celebrations, which include lively music, dance, and Vodou rituals.

Vodou items for
sale at a market in
Santo Domingo.

that are said to possess humans. The spiritual leaders also perform a divination ritual called *fa-a*. In this ritual, a hungan or
mambo scatters palm kernels on a cloth. The way they land is
interpreted to predict the future and solve problems.

Although no religion is illegal in the Dominican Republic,
Vodou can be socially unpopular. Some people consider it anti-
Catholic or look down on those who practice it. Because of
this, many people who follow Vodou keep their beliefs secret.
Despite this, Vodou products can be found in markets through-
out the country, in part to satisfy the curiosity of tourists.

CHAPTER 9

Color and Sound

THE DOMINICAN REPUBLIC'S DIVERSE POPULATION has given the island a unique and lively culture. The native Taíno people had a rich culture of story, music, and art. As groups of Spaniards, Africans, and others came to live there, they brought new customs and arts that blended into today's way of life.

Opposite: **The guitar is an important instrument in bachata, a type of music that originated in the Dominican Republic.**

Folk Arts

Some traditional Taíno crafts have endured, especially those using the calabash gourd. A gourd is a hard-shelled fruit of a plant such as a squash or melon. After the gourd is dried, it is carved to make containers, masks, and musical instruments such as maracas. These crafts persist throughout the island, in part because of tourism. Many visitors look for handmade items to bring home as souvenirs.

Pottery made of a reddish terra-cotta clay is very popular in the Dominican Republic. Some pieces are very simple while others are made with fine details. Among the most popular pottery products are nativity sets for Christmas. These sets depict the story of Jesus's birth in a stable, complete with animals such as sheep and donkeys. Elsewhere in the world, nativity sets usually include camels, but in the Dominican Republic they often show cows instead.

Dominican artisans make pots, plates, and more out of clay.

Some tourists shops for macramé when they're on vacation in the Dominican Republic. Macramé can be made at home without special equipment. It involves knotting twine or

Oscar de la Renta poses with a model wearing one of dresses.

Easy Elegance

Oscar de la Renta, one of the world's greatest fashion designers, was born into a prominent family in Santo Domingo in 1932. At age eighteen, he moved to Spain to study art, and his sketches of dresses were soon gaining attention. He worked for other prominent designers before starting his own company in 1965.

De la Renta's designs were relaxed, modern, romantic, and elegant. He became known for dressing style icons such as former first lady Jacqueline Kennedy Onassis. By the time he died in 2014, he had designed dresses for five first ladies and countless movie stars.

cords into a netlike pattern. Macramé is often done by women and children, especially in rural areas. It can be used to create a wide variety of products, including purses, shopping bags, and hammocks.

Other crafts as well, such as palm weaving, require few tools and can be done using low-cost resources. For example,

Some Dominican painters create colorful works that they sell to tourists.

many craftspeople close to the coast use coral and seashells to create beautiful jewelry that is sold to tourists. These crafts provide much-needed income to families.

Visual Arts

The Dominican Republic has a rich tradition of fine arts, especially painting. Jaime Colson was one of the nation's leading artistic figures of the twentieth century. He worked in many different modern art styles, including cubism, where images are broken apart into geometric shapes, and expressionism, where artists paint the emotional experience of what they see. Celeste Woss y Gil, a contemporary of Colson, was the first female artist in the Dominican Republic to have a solo show. She shocked some people in Santo Domingo with her paintings of naked women.

Woss y Gil was one of the founders of the National School of Fine Arts, where many younger painters trained. One of her students there was Clara Ledesma, one of the Dominican

Republic's greatest artists. Her work is known for its rich colors and almost magical quality.

Some Dominican artists have explored media beyond painting. In addition to his work as a painter and sculptor, José Rincón Mora designed the stained glass windows for St. James the Apostle Cathedral in Santiago.

Literature

Like other aspects of Dominican life, its literature has been influenced by many different cultures. Until recent times, only the wealthy could afford an education, so the nation's writers

A painting by Clara Ledesma is displayed at an auction.

Juan Bosch: Writer and Politician

Juan Bosch is known for being the first democratically elected president of the Dominican Republic. But he was far more than a politician. Bosch, who was born in 1909, became concerned with human rights after Rafael Trujillo came to power in 1930. He wrote many essays, which resulted in him being exiled when he was twenty-six years old. He continued to write about politics and social issues. His ability to express himself in writing helped others recognize the important issues facing their nation.

Bosch also wrote many short stories, including "The Masters" and "Luis Pié," that dealt with social issues. They are considered among the greatest short stories by a Latin American author. Bosch died in 2001, after a long life devoted to helping his country.

Juan Bosch wrote more than thirty books, including fiction, history, and essays.

have historically been from the upper class. As the middle class grows, the country's literature is beginning to represent a broader group.

Salomé Ureña, a prominent writer of the nineteenth century, was known for her poetry, some tragic, some tender. She was also involved in broader cultural affairs. She helped open the first institution for higher education for women in the Dominican Republic. Her son Pedro Henríquez Ureña became a well-known philosopher and literary critic. Salomé Ureña and Pedro Henríquez Ureña appear together on the 500 Dominican peso banknote.

Some of the country's best-known writers have been active in politics. Former president Juan Bosch is one of the greatest, noted for his political essays and short stories. Joaquín Balaguer, also a Dominican president, wrote poetry.

Many younger Dominican writers have one foot in the Dominican Republic and the other in the United States. Julia Alvarez was born in New York City but then spent much of her childhood in the Dominican Republic. She has written many acclaimed novels, including *How the García Girls Lost Their Accents*. It tells of sisters living in New York City looking back on their childhood during the Trujillo dictatorship. Another of her novels, *Before We Were Free*, explores life under Trujillo through the eyes of a twelve-year-old.

The works of Julia Alvarez explore questions of cultural identity.

The music of Juan Luis Guerra mixes merengue, Afro-Latin music, jazz, and other styles.

Other Dominican writers who have written about the immigrant experience include Junot Díaz, whose novel *The Brief Wondrous Life of Oscar Wao* won the Pulitzer Prize in Fiction.

Music and Dance

The Dominican Republic is a land rich in music. The most popular type of music is merengue, which shows both African and Spanish influences. Traditional instruments used to play merengue include a two-ended drum called a *tambora*, the accordion, and the *güira*, a metal percussion instrument that makes a scraping sound. In the 1900s, other instruments were added to the merengue sound, including saxophone, guitar, flute, and maracas. When dancing to merengue, partners hold each other close. The upper body is kept still, while the dancers move in small steps.

The Dominican Republic has produced many great merengue musicians. These include Johnny Ventura, who later became mayor of Santo Domingo, and Milly Quezada, who is known as the Queen of Merengue. The most acclaimed of all is Juan Luis Guerra. As a composer, he is famed for his innovative mixture of different influences. By 2018, he had sold more than thirty million records worldwide.

Guerra helped popularize bachata, another type of Dominican music and dance, around the world. The lyrics in bachata music are often about heartbreak, and dancers move from side to side or in a box pattern with a strong tap on the fourth beat.

A merengue band includes an accordian and a güira. The güira is made of metal and played with a brush.

Dominicans perform and enjoy many other kinds of music as well. Toque Profundo is one of the most popular Dominican rock bands. Rap has become hugely popular. Top Dominican rappers include Lapiz Conciente and Yo Yais. Many Dominicans also listen to punk, heavy metal, and jazz.

Play Ball!

Sports are an important part of life for many people in the Dominican Republic. The nation has been sending athletes to the Olympics since 1964. Dominicans have won medals in track and field, boxing, and tae kwon do.

Many Dominicans enjoy

A woman shows off her merengue skills by dancing on a bottle.

playing soccer, basketball, and volleyball. But the sport that Dominicans are most passionate about is baseball. The sport was introduced to the nation in 1891 by neighboring Cubans, who had learned the sport from American soldiers. At first, plantation owners encouraged the sport to keep workers occupied during the slow seasons. Its popularity spread, and by the 1920s a Dominican baseball league was springing to life.

About 1,100 players from the Dominican Republic have been on the Major League rosters in the U.S. and Canada. Although there are many theories as to how this tiny country became so important to the sport of baseball, it is easy to see how it is able to keep Dominican players rising.

All Major League Baseball clubs now have training facilities in the Dominican Republic where they host young

Dominican kids play volleyball on the beach.

David Ortiz ended his Major League Baseball career with 541 home runs.

The Best at Bat

David Ortiz is one of the greatest Dominican Major League Baseball players of all time. Born in Santo Domingo in 1975, he was inspired by his father who was a player in the Dominican leagues. American scouts spotted Ortiz at a young age, and at sixteen he was recruited to play in the minor leagues. He began his twenty-year Major League career at age twenty-one with the Minnesota Twins. In 2003, he moved to the Boston Red Sox, where he would spend the rest of his career.

Ortiz, who was famed for his powerful hitting, helped the Red Sox win three World Series championships. He was named to the All-Star team ten times, and over the course of his career hit more than five hundred home runs.

hopefuls. Kids at the training facilities want to learn, practice, and hopefully get spotted by a scout. Playing professional baseball is the dream of many Dominican boys who have grown up hearing not just about the fame and money the players earn but also the work they have done to help their country.

Pitcher Pedro Martinez helped rebuild the neighborhood he grew up in, and sluggers Albert Pujols and David Ortiz have major charity organizations. To be a Major League Baseball player is to be a national hero.

Out of the thousands of kids who try to make it as a baseball player, only a small percentage have a chance of making it big. Many youngsters quit school to join a training program. Those who don't succeed are left with no education to fall back on. Some people criticize the teams for giving vulnerable kids false hope, but others see any opportunity as positive.

A Dominican boy focuses as he prepares to hit the ball.

CHAPTER 10

Everyday Life

FAMILY BONDS ARE VERY STRONG IN THE DOMINICAN Republic. Here, family includes not just parents, children, and grandparents but more distant relatives and in-laws. Members of the extended family have a responsibility to be there for each other, joining together in times of need to help in whatever way they can. This is true of everyone, from the poorest family to the wealthiest. It is the reason that so many Dominicans who have moved abroad send money back home to support the family they left behind.

Godparents, called *compadres*, are also a very important part of the family unit. While a godparent is often more symbolic in the United States and Canada, in the Dominican Republic the compadre takes on a great deal of responsibility. When people agree to the role, they are pledging that they will be a part of the child's upbringing, especially in relation to

Opposite: **A fisherman heads out into the sea.**

major religious events. The compadre is expected to help pay for the child's baptism ceremony, marriage, and even funeral. The parents or child may also ask the compadre for money to help with medical bills, school, and other costs.

Home Sweet Home

Family homes in the Dominican Republic vary tremendously. In larger cities like Santo Domingo, those with good-paying jobs might have an apartment or their own house just outside the city. Many people who live in the city but make little

Funeral Traditions

Traditionally, when a person dies, the whole family gathers by the deceased and stays until the next day's funeral. The nine days following the death are a time of mourning called *la novena*. During this time, people come together at the home to pray for the soul of the deceased and talk about the good that person brought into the world while on earth.

money live in shacks that may not be much more than a cardboard box. These provide shelter but little comfort.

In the countryside, some people live in huts made of bamboo and palm leaves. Sometimes other materials are added to the huts to make them sturdier. Plaster and stones might be added to the walls or sheets of zinc or tin could be used as a roof. Some rural shacks have cement floors, while others have dirt.

Some people in rural areas build wooden houses. These might be occupied by many members of an extended family and are often painted with bright colors.

Family members sit outside their house. The average family in the Dominican Republic has two children.

Getting Around

Wealthier Dominicans use cars to get from place to place. Many other people ride motor scooters or bikes. In the city, many people take buses, which can get very crowded. In rural areas, people tend to share vehicles or pay for a ride only when they need it. Pickup trucks and vans are often packed with people headed to and from work. People going shorter distances walk.

Fantastic Food

Typical Dominican foods are made from ingredients that are grown easily. Along the coast, many people rely on the sea as a source of food. Common fish used in meals are cod, grouper, and tuna. The most common shellfish is conch, which is often made into fritters. Coconut is often used to sweeten seafood dishes.

Starchy vegetables are a large part of the Dominican diet. These include root vegetables like taro and yams. Plantains are used in many recipes and are a favorite breakfast food. Plantains look like bananas, but they have thicker skins, are not as sweet, and they need to be cooked before they are eaten. The most popular plantain dish is a fried patty called a tostone.

Many people in the Dominican Republic use scooters to get around town.

Tostones are eaten both as a street food and as a side dish.

Making Tostones

Also known as twice-fried plantains, tostones are as common a side dish in the Dominican Republic as French fries are in the United States. They are quick to prepare and will disappear even more quickly. Have an adult help you with this recipe.

Ingredients
2 plantains
3/4 cup vegetable oil
Salt to taste

Directions
Peel the plantains, and cut them into one-inch-long sections. Pour the oil into a large frying pan, and heat it over medium-high heat. When the oil is hot, place the plantain pieces in the pan and fry them until they are golden brown. Be sure to turn them to cook both sides.

When they are done cooking, remove them from the oil and place them on a plate lined with paper towels to soak up the oil. Place one piece at a time on a cutting board, and use the bottom of a coffee mug to press it flat. When all the pieces have been flattened, put the plantains back in the oil, and fry on both sides until the edges are crisp. Place the tostones on a fresh paper towel and sprinkle them with salt. Then enjoy!

Beans are an important source of protein in the Dominican diet. Eggs are also used as a protein, and are typically served at dinner. Goat, pork, and chicken are the most commonly eaten meats. They are usually cooked in soups and stews. Roast pig is the traditional dish at Christmas feasts, and fish is traditionally served on Easter. On Independence Day, Dominicans eat a stew called *la bandera* (the flag), made of rice, beans, and meat. The red beans and white rice represent the country's flag.

Dominicans usually drink dark-roast coffee with lots of sugar.

Having Fun

Dominican people work hard, so they look forward to time off. Gathering with family and friends is a favorite way to relax at the end of the day. Often, people gather for a meal. On Sundays, it is common for several families to get together to enjoy games, music, and food while the children play.

Music and dance are favorite pastimes. People often dance in public when street musicians are playing. In cities, whole blocks might become a dance floor on a Friday or Saturday night. Cities also have dance clubs, and most restaurants have music and a place to dance. In rural areas, the center of town might fill with dancers if someone pulls out an instrument or a radio.

National Holidays

New Year's Day	January 1
Epiphany	January 6
Our Lady of Altagracia Day	January 21
Duarte's Day	January 29
Independence Day	February 27
Good Friday	March or April
Labor Day	May 1
Corpus Christi	May or June
Restoration Day	August 16
Our Lady of Mercy Day	September 24
Constitution Day	November 5
Christmas Day	December 25

A young man dressed as Santa Claus entertains children at a Christmas fair in Santo Domingo.

Party Time

Dance is also a part of many festivals in the Dominican Republic. Carnival, the nation's biggest festival, is held just before the beginning of Lent, a solemn stretch of forty days that Catholics observe before Easter. Santo Domingo's Carnival is the country's biggest, but the celebration is held in

A man carves a mask for Carnival.

every city. The centerpiece of Carnival is a huge parade filled with floats and people wearing elaborate costumes that they have spent weeks making.

The most popular costume is a representation of a creature called the *diablo cojuelo*. The creature, which has huge horns and rows of sharp teeth, is said to have the power to rid the body of evil. Many spectators, especially children, make masks of the diablo's face. Carnival also includes groups of women who do a whirling dance in long white dresses with wide skirts. Around them dance *la Muerte Enjipe*, a group of men who wear black suits painted with skeletons. All along the path of the parade are musicians playing merengue and street vendors selling food and souvenirs. In the Dominican Republic, the party goes on for two full days and nights, and then it is time to rest.

A young girl wears a lion costume during the La Vega Carnival.

Timeline

Dominican History

4000 to 3000 BCE
The first people arrive on Hispaniola.

Late 1400s
Carib people attack Taínos on Hispaniola.

ca. 1400s
About half a million Taínos live on Hispaniola.

1492
The first Europeans arrive on Hispaniola.

1496
Santo Domingo is founded.

1538
A university is established in Santo Domingo.

Mid-1500s
Spain loses interest in Hispaniola.

1791
Black slaves in western Hispaniola revolt in the Haitian Revolution and take over the entire island.

1809
Spanish-speaking colonists in eastern Hispaniola reunite with Spain.

1821
The colony declares independence, calling itself Spanish Haiti.

1822
Haitian troops invade and occupy Spanish Haiti.

1844
Rebels defeat Haitian troops and declare the Dominican Republic independent.

1861
The Dominican Republic becomes a Spanish colony to protect it from Haitian attack.

1865
The Dominican Republic becomes independent again.

| 5000 | BCE 0 CE | 1000 | 1400 | 1500 | 1700 | 1800 | 1850 |

World History

ca. 2500 BCE
The Egyptians build the pyramids and the Sphinx in Giza.

ca. 563 BCE
The Buddha is born in India.

313 CE
The Roman emperor Constantine legalizes Christianity.

610
The Prophet Muhammad begins preaching a new religion called Islam.

1054
The Eastern (Orthodox) and Western (Roman Catholic) Churches break apart.

1095
The Crusades begin.

1215
King John seals the Magna Carta.

1300s
The Renaissance begins in Italy.

1347
The plague sweeps through Europe.

1453
Ottoman Turks capture Constantinople, conquering the Byzantine Empire.

1492
Columbus arrives in North America.

1500s
Reformers break away from the Catholic Church, and Protestantism is born.

1776
The U.S. Declaration of Independence is signed.

1789
The French Revolution begins.

1865
The American Civil War ends.

1879
The first practical lightbulb is invente

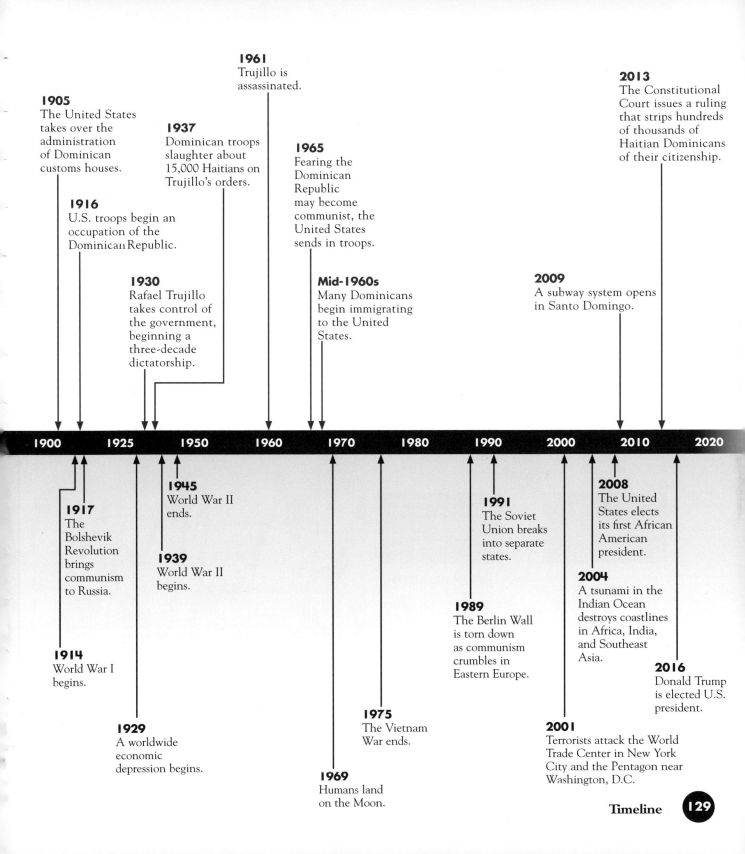

1905
The United States takes over the administration of Dominican customs houses.

1916
U.S. troops begin an occupation of the Dominican Republic.

1937
Dominican troops slaughter about 15,000 Haitians on Trujillo's orders.

1961
Trujillo is assassinated.

1965
Fearing the Dominican Republic may become communist, the United States sends in troops.

2013
The Constitutional Court issues a ruling that strips hundreds of thousands of Haitian Dominicans of their citizenship.

1930
Rafael Trujillo takes control of the government, beginning a three-decade dictatorship.

Mid-1960s
Many Dominicans begin immigrating to the United States.

2009
A subway system opens in Santo Domingo.

1900   1925   1950   1960   1970   1980   1990   2000   2010   2020

1917
The Bolshevik Revolution brings communism to Russia.

1945
World War II ends.

1991
The Soviet Union breaks into separate states.

2008
The United States elects its first African American president.

1914
World War I begins.

1939
World War II begins.

1989
The Berlin Wall is torn down as communism crumbles in Eastern Europe.

2004
A tsunami in the Indian Ocean destroys coastlines in Africa, India, and Southeast Asia.

2016
Donald Trump is elected U.S. president.

1929
A worldwide economic depression begins.

1975
The Vietnam War ends.

2001
Terrorists attack the World Trade Center in New York City and the Pentagon near Washington, D.C.

1969
Humans land on the Moon.

Timeline

Fast Facts

Official name of the country: Dominican Republic

Capital: Santo Domingo

Official language: Spanish

Year of independence: 1844

National anthem: "Himno Nacional"

Type of government: Presidential republic

Head of state: President

Head of government: President

Left to right: **National flag, presidential guard**

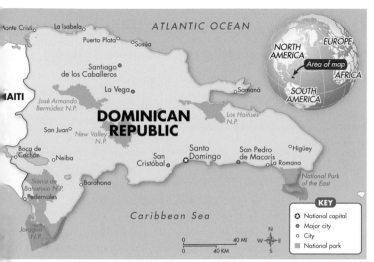

Los Haitises National Park

Area of country:	18,816 square miles (48,734 sq km)
Latitude and longitude of country's geographic center:	19°00' N, 70°40' W
Bordering country:	Haiti to the west
Highest elevation:	Duarte Peak, 10,417 feet (3,175 m) above sea level
Lowest elevation:	Lake Enriquillo, 112 feet (34 m) below sea level
Average high temperature:	87°F (31°C) in July
Average low temperature:	67°F (19°C) in January
Average annual precipitation:	100 inches (250 cm) in higher elevations, 40 inches (100 cm) in lower elevations

National population (2018 est.):	10,914,696	
Population of major cities:	Santo Domingo	2,908,607
	Santiago de los Caballeros	553,091
	La Vega	210,736
	San Cristóbal	209,165
	San Pedro de Macorís	205,911

Landmarks:
▶ *Cathedral of Santa María la Menor,* Santo Domingo

▶ *Monument to the Heroes of the Restoration,* Santiago

▶ *New Valley National Park,* Constanza

▶ *Ozama Fortress,* Santo Domingo

▶ *Shrine of Our Lady of Altagracia,* Higüey

Economy: Service industries employ approximately two-thirds of the workforce. Finance, trade, and tourism are major parts of the service sector of the economy. Each year more than six million people visit the country. Mining is a smaller industry, with gold the most profitable product. The Dominican Republic has free trade zones, where foreign manufacturing companies can do business without paying import and export taxes. These companies employ about 140,000 Dominican workers. Major crops grown in the Dominican Republic include sugarcane, tobacco, cocoa beans, bananas, and many kinds of vegetables.

Currency: The Dominican peso. In 2018, 1 Dominican peso equaled 2¢, and 50 Dominican pesos equaled $1.

System of weights and measures: Officially, the metric system is used, but day-to-day use is a mixture of metric and American customary units.

Literacy rate: 92%

Spanish words and phrases:		
Hola	Hello	
Adiós	Good-bye	
Buenos días	Good morning	
Buenas noches	Good evening	
Por favor	Please	
Gracias	Thank you	
De nada	You're welcome	

Prominent Dominicans:

Julia Alvarez	(1950–)
Novelist	
Juan Bosch	(1909–2001)
Politician and short story writer	
Oscar de la Renta	(1932–2014)
Clothing designer	
Juan Pablo Duarte	(1813–1876)
Father of Dominican independence	
Fabio Fiallo	(1866–1942)
Poet and politician	
Juan Luis Guerra	(1957–)
Composer and singer	
David Ortiz	(1975–)
Baseball player	
Salomé Ureña	(1850–1897)
Poet and advocate for women's education	

Clockwise from top: **Currency, David Ortiz, schoolchildren**

To Find Out More

Books

▶ Alvarez, Julia. *Before We Were Free*. New York: Knopf, 2002.

▶ Ferguson, James. *Top 10: Dominican Republic*. New York: Dorling Kindersley, 2015.

▶ Tavares, Matt. *Growing Up Pedro*. Somerville, MA: Candlewick, 2017.

Music

▶ Guerra, Juan Luis. *A Son de Guerra*. Los Angeles: Capitol Latin, 2010.

▶ *Rough Guide to Merengue & Bachata*. London: World Music Network, 2001.

▶ Visit this Scholastic website for more information on Dominican Republic:
www.factsfornow.scholastic.com
Enter the keywords **Dominican Republic**

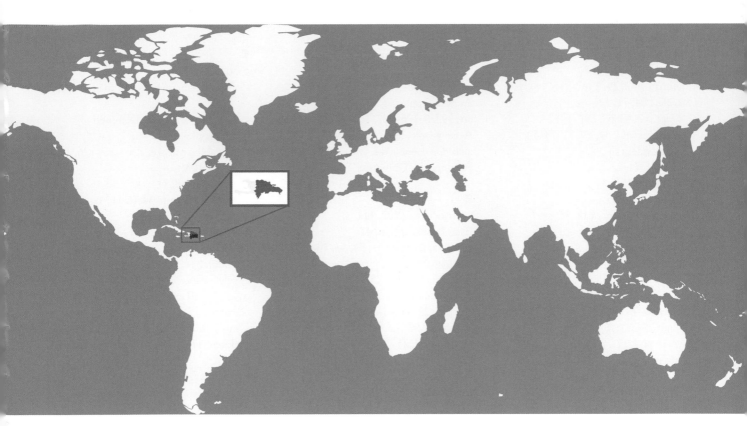

Location of the Dominican Republic

Index

Page numbers in *italics* indicate illustrations.

J

Jaragua National Park, 31
jewelry, 16, *73*, 74
Johnson, Lyndon B., 56
José Armando Bermúdez National Park, 31
Judaism, 97
judicial branch of government, 61, 63, 65

L

La Isabela settlement, 41
Lake Enriquillo, 18, *18*, 19, 20, 29
Lake Saumâtre, 19
La Navidad settlement, 40
languages, 64, 87–88, *87*, 89
Lapiz Conciente, 112
larimar mining, 73–74, *73*
La Romana, 21
La Vega, 22, 80, *127*
Ledesma, Clara, 106–107, *107*
legislative branch of government, 61–62
literature, 50, 107–110, *108*, 133
livestock, 18, 35, 51, 72–73, 123
Los Haitises National Park, 30, 31, *31*
Louverture, Toussaint, *46*

M

macramé, 104–105
mambos (Vodou spiritual leaders), 100, 101
mangoes, 34, *34*, 72
mangrove trees, 30, *30*
manufacturing, 74–77, *75*
maps. *See also* historical maps.
    geopolitical, *10*
    population density, *80*
    provinces, *65*
    resources, *71*
    Santo Domingo, *66*
    topographical, *20*
marine life, 24, 29, 30–32, *32*, 120–121

marketplaces, 101, *101*
marriages, 92, 93, 98, 118
Martinez, Pedro, 115
Medina, Danilo, 57, 63
Mejía, Hipólito, 57
merengue music, 110–111, *110*, *111*, *112*, 127
military, 47, 54, 56, 58, 60, *64*, 67
mining, 39, 51, 57, 73–75, *73*
Mirabel sisters, 77
Modern Revolutionary Party (PRM), 59
mongooses, 35, *35*
Monte Cristi, 16
Monument to the Heroes of the Restoration, 22, *22*
mosquitoes, 16, *16*
mudslides, 24, 25
la Muerte Enjipe (dancers), 127
music, 64, *64*, *102*, 110–112, *110*, *111*, 124

N

national anthem, 64
national bird, 33, *33*
national coat of arms, 60
National Congress, 61–62, 65
National Council of the Judiciary, 63
National District, 65
national flag, 60, *60*, 123
national flower, 29
national holidays, 10, 125
national motto, 60
national name, 60
National Palace, 62
National Pantheon, 50
National Park of the East, 31
national parks, 27–28, *30*, 31, *31*
National School of Fine Arts, 106
Neiba Mountains, 19
newspapers, 50
New Valley National Park, 27–28
Neiba Valley, 19

North River. *See* Yaque del Norte.
la novena (time of mourning), 119

O

Old Spanish language, 88
Olympic Games, 112
oraciones (superstitions), 98
orchids, 31
Organization of American States (OAS), 53, 54
Ortiz, David, 114, *114*, 115, 133, *133*
Our Lady of Altagracia, 94, *94*
Ovando, Nicolás de, 43
Ozama Fortress, 42
Ozama River, *49*, 66

P

palmchat (national bird), 33, *33*
Panama Canal, 48
papayas, 40, *40*
pectolite mining, *73*
Peña Gómez, José Francisco, 56
people
    ancestors, 79–80, 81
    Arawak, 37
    Asians, 80, 88, 97
    average age, 79
    blanco, 81
    Carib, 37, 39–40
    children, *11*, *24*, 85, 105, *120*, *125*, 127, *127*
    citizenship, 82, *82*
    clothing, *92*, 98, 105, *105*, 133
    compadres (godparents), 117–118
    diseases, 44, 47
    early people, 37
    education, 51, 85–87, *85*, 93, 107, 115
    emigration, 56, 83–85, *84*
    employment, *57*, 70, 72, *72*, 75–76, *81*, 85, 86
    encomienda system, 41

Meet the Authors

BARBARA RADCLIFFE ROGERS HAS BEEN A WRITER AND EDITOR since her college days. After working as a speechwriter for senators and congresspeople in Washington, D.C., she moved on to writing on subjects ranging from travel to food to folk arts. She is the coauthor of more than thirty guidebooks on places such as Italy, Portugal, Spain, Germany, and Canada. Introducing young readers to the world is especially important to her, and she has written many books on countries and cities of the world.

Having spent her youth accompanying her parents on their own professional travel-writing adventures, Lura Rogers Seavey developed a love for travel at an early age. Today, she continues the family tradition by exploring the world with her own children and sharing her enthusiasm and experiences with readers. In addition to authoring many titles in Scholastic's Enchantment of the World series, she writes for many travel publications.

Photo Credits

Photographs ©: cover: Jane Sweeney/Getty Images; back cover: Hans Neleman/Getty Images; 2: Wayne Walton/Getty Images; 4 left: Jane Sweeney/Getty Images; 4 center: Candace Barbot/Miami Herald/MCT/Getty Images; 4 right: Jane Sweeney/Getty Images;5 left: EFE/Orlando Barria/Alamy Images; 5 right: Stephen Frink/Getty Images; 6: Lucas Vallecillos/Alamy Images; 8: Soberka Richard/age fotostock; 9: Jane Sweeney/Getty Images; 11: Gardel Bertrand/age fotostock; 12: Luciano Ippolito/iStockphoto; 14: The History Collection/Alamy Images; 15: Jane Sweeney/Getty Images; 16: VPC Travel Photo/Alamy Images; 17: Moirenc Camille/age fotostock; 18: Sergii Batechenkov/iStockphoto; 19: Francesco Tomasinelli/age fotostock; 21: Jane Sweeney/Getty Images; 22 top right: Hackenberg-Photo-Cologne/Alamy Images; 22 bottom left: Soberka Richard/hemis.fr/Getty Images; 23: Erika Santelices/AFP/GettyImages; 24: kate_sept2004/Getty Images; 25: Keystone-France/Gamma-Keystone/Getty Images; 26: Kevin Schafer/Getty Images; 28: Yann Arthus-Bertrand/Getty Images; 29: Kevin Schafer/Minden Pictures; 30: Hackenberg-Photo-Cologne/Alamy Images; 31 top right: Neil Bowman/Minden Pictures; 31 bottom left: Daniela Dirscherl/Getty Images; 32: Stephen Frink/Getty Images; 33: Neil Bowman/Minden Pictures; 34: Marvin del Cid/Getty Images; 35: Phil Degginger/age fotostock; 36: Timothy O'Keefe/Getty Images; 38: Musee de l'Homme, Paris, France/Bridgeman Images; 39: DEA/V. Giannella/Getty Images; 40: Sir Pengallan/age fotostock; 42: Christophe Boisvieux/Getty Images; 43: DEA/Bibloteca Ambrosiana/Getty Images; 44: Lebrecht Music & Arts/Alamy Images; 46: Historic Images/Alamy Images; 49: Interim Archives/Getty Images; 50: Fabio Darío Herrera/Wikimedia; 52: Hulton Archive/Getty Images; 53: Tony Savino/Corbis/Getty Images; 54: Lynn Pelham/The LIFE Images Collection/Getty Images; 55: Hulton-Deutsch Collection/Corbis/Getty Images; 57: Robert Nickelsberg/Getty Images; 58: Tony Savino/Corbis/Getty Images; 60: Asuwan Masae/Shutterstock; 62: Peter Schickert/age fotostock; 63: Fran Afonso/Xinhua/Alamy Images; 64: Peter Schickert/age fotostock; 66 top: Jane Sweeney/Getty Images; 67: Erika Santelices/AFP/Getty Images; 68: Kennet Havgaard/Aurora Photos; 70: Escudero Patrick/age fotostock; 72: Javier Teniente/Cover/Getty Images; 73: Evannovostro/Shutterstock; 75: Walter Bibikow/Danita Delimont Stock Photography; 76: Robert Nickelsberg/Getty Images; 77: Glyn Thomas/Alamy Images; 78: Candace Barbot/Miami Herald/MCT/Getty Images; 81: Erika Santelices/AFP/Getty Images; 82: Santiago Vidal/LatinContent Getty Images; 83: Erika Santelices/AFP/Getty Images; 84: Enid Alvarez/NY Daily News/Getty Images; 85: Education & Exploration 4/Alamy Images; 86: RosalreneBetancourt 12/Alamy Images; 87: Irène Alastruey/age fotostock; 88: Erika Santelices/AFP/Getty Images; 89: Jane Sweeney/AWL Images; 90: Fran Afonso/Xinhua/Alamy Images; 92: Alvaro Leiva/age fotostock; 94: CSP_demerzel21/age fotostock; 95: EFE/Orlando Barria/Alamy Images; 96: Paul Jeffrey/kairosphotos.com; 97: Anadolu Agency/Getty Images; 99: Dallas Stribley/Getty Images; 100: Erika Santelices/AFP/Getty Images; 101: James Quine/Alamy Images; 102: Margie Politzer/Getty Images; 104: Donald Nausbaum/Alamy Images; 105: Jean-Claude Deutsch/Paris Match/Getty Images; 106: Wayne Walton/Getty Images; 107: Orlando Barria/Epa/Shutterstock; 108: Bettmann/Getty Images; 109: Ramon Espinosa/AP Images; 110: Nick Pickles/Wirelmage/Getty Images; 111: Carl & Ann Purcell/Getty Images; 112: Jon McLean/Alamy Images; 113: Jane Sweeney/Getty Images; 114: Michael Ivins/Boston Red Sox/Getty Images; 115: Ronald C. Modra/Sports Imagery/Getty Images; 116: Moirenc Camille/age fotostock; 118: Melanie Stetson Freeman/The Christian Science Monitor/Getty Images; 119: Michael Dwyer/Alamy Images; 120: Jane Sweeney/Getty Images; 121: Jane Sweeney/Getty Images; 122: Ildi Papp/Shutterstock; 123: RosalreneBetancourt 9/Alamy Images; 124: Giovanni Tagini/Alamy Images; 125: Erika Santelices/AFP/Getty Images; 126: VPC Photo/Alamy Images; 127: Jon G. Fuller/VW Pics/UIG/Getty Images; 130 left: Asuwan Masae/Shutterstock; 130 right: Tony Savino/Corbis/Getty Images; 131 right: Daniela Dirscherl/Getty Images; 133 center left: Glyn Thomas/Alamy Images; 133 bottom left: Education & Exploration 4/Alamy Images; 133 bottom right: Michael Ivins/Boston Red Sox/Getty Images.

Maps by Mapping Specialists.